TEACHING SOCIAL STUDIES THAT MATTERS

Curriculum for Active Learning

TEACHING SOCIAL STUDIES THAT MATTERS

Curriculum for Active Learning

Stephen J. Thornton

Foreword by Nel Noddings

Teachers College, Columbia University
New York and London

Published by Teachers College Press, 1234 Amsterdam Avenue, New York, NY 10027

Library of Congress Cataloging-in-Publication Data

Thronton, Stephen J.
  Social studies that matters: Curriculum for active learning / Stephen J. Thornton
    p. cm.
  Includes bibliographical references and index.
  ISBN 0-8077-4523-5 (cloth : alk. paper) — ISBN 0-8077-4522-7 (pbk. : alk. paper)
  1. Social sciences—Study and teaching (Elementary)—United States—Curricula. 2. Social sciences—Study and teaching (Secondary)—United States—Curricula. 3. Curriculum planning—United States. I. Title.

LB1584.T47 2004
300'.71—dc22   2004053730

ISBN 0-8077-4522-7 (paper)
ISBN 0-8077-4523-5 (cloth)

Printed on acid-free paper

Manufactured in the United States of America

12 11 10 09 08 07 06 05   8 7 6 5 4 3 2 1

Contents

Foreword

In this important book, Steve Thornton brings a Deweyan perspective to current problems in social studies education. He does more than this, however, because his analysis can be extended profitably to every subject in the curriculum.

He reminds us that the choices educators must make on topics, methods, conceptual understandings, and skills are basically *educational* questions, not merely questions to be answered from the perspective of a particular discipline. It is hard to exaggerate the importance of this reminder. Too often curriculum-makers have allowed subject-matter experts to decide on topics, conceptual understandings, and skills—leaving only the choice of pedagogical methods to teachers. This has certainly been the case in mathematics, the school subject I know best, and it seems to be true in other fields as well. In acquiescing to this arrangement, we seem to forget that all of these choices should be made with respect to overarching educational aims and that these aims are established and continually evaluated with careful consideration of individual and societal needs, the nature of human flourishing, and the effects of human activity in the natural world.

Curricula established entirely by subject-matter experts are often of little interest to the majority of students. Almost by definition, such curricula aim at preparing students to "think like" mathematicians, historians, biologists, artists, and so on. Too little thought is given to how students can use the material in their own present and future lives. Because students so often perceive the material generated by subject-matter experts as irrelevant, teachers are continually forced to motivate students. Thornton follows Dewey in advising us that the existing motivation of students can often be used to construct powerful lessons and units of study.

Another pernicious effect of overdependence on subject-matter experts is that teachers are judged by how closely they resemble the expert disciplinary model. Mathematicians rarely acknowledge high school mathematics teachers as mathematicians, for example, but a common attitude evaluates teachers on the basis of how nearly they approximate that model. The attitude implicitly describes K–12 teachers as deficient. I am not arguing that specific subject-matter knowledge is unimportant for teachers; I believe it is very important. But K–12 teachers do not need the higher math created and used by mathematicians. Instead, they need a broad knowledge of many subjects so that they can make educationally adequate choices of the sort that Thornton has described. (Note that "mathematician" can be replaced in this paragraph by "historian," "scientist," or other professions.)

Again, neither Thornton nor I would leave subject-matter experts out of curriculum making. Their role (once their subject has been chosen—and that is a matter beyond discussion here) is essential, but it is subordinate to those who, cooperatively, establish the great, guiding aims of education. Mathematicians and historians can tell us what is important within their subjects, how topics might best be ordered, and what skills seem to be necessary in developing understanding of central concepts. These are important functions.

Throughout his book, Thornton argues for the integration of skills and content, content and method, content and sources. Should skills or content drive the curriculum? Thornton's sensible answer is "neither." When skills, such as critical thinking, are intimately connected to educational aims, they do deserve priority and, when that priority is recognized, teachers should have wide latitude in the choice of content to develop those skills. But that does not mean that one bit of content is as good as any other. Some content—for example, the development of democracy as a political system and way of life—is crucially important and must be central in a social studies curriculum. But how do we select particular topics from this broad area of content and how do we arrange study of the topics so that the essential skills we have identified will also be promoted?

Even with these questions answered, the teacher's task as curricular gatekeeper is not finished. He or she must decide which facts associated with the content are essential and which are incidental. Constant care must be taken to prevent what so often happens in social studies courses—a steady deterioration into mindless memorization of facts. Students cannot engage in critical thinking without adequate background knowledge in the area of study. But how much knowledge is required? Exactly what does that knowledge consist of? And what should come next?

Because social studies teachers in the United States are responsible for helping students to prepare for life in a liberal democracy, they must also involve students in some of these choices. When an array of appropriate topics has been identified, students should be invited to choose among them. Having the opportunity to choose is important in itself because of its connection to motivation, but the educational aim in a liberal democracy should be to help students make well-informed choices. What problem interests the student? How will study of this topic contribute both to understanding the problem and to the student's growth as a participant in our democratic way of life?

The teacher's job requires constant attention to continuity. A problem-centered approach, for example, does not imply leaping from problem to problem without regard for how topics, skills, methods, and conceptual understandings are connected and related to educational aims. Thornton makes all of these connections central to the work of social studies teachers.

I have long believed that no subject in the school curriculum is more important than social studies because it involves us most directly in the study of our earth as the home of human activity and the effects of that activity on all life. It also encourages us to think more deeply about the kinds of activity that may preserve both earth and life. Thornton's book has strengthened that belief.

Nel Noddings

Acknowledgments

I am indebted to more people than I can presently recall for conversations that were helpful in writing this book. I am grateful to them all. Fortunately, I can be more specific about some debts. The late Richard E. Gross was characteristically supportive about the idea for this book, and conversations with Keith Barton and Ruth Vinz stimulated my thinking. Ellen Livingston and Ben Jacobs provided capable research assistance. Nancy Brickhouse, Margaret Smith Crocco, David Flinders, and Linda Levstik generously spent time commenting on early drafts of parts of the manuscript. I am particularly grateful to Jane White for providing detailed and incisive feedback on the first sections of the manuscript. Her encouragement, along with that of two anonymous reviewers, helped me see this book through to the finish. Whatever faults remain are my responsibility alone. It was a pleasure to work with my editor, Brian Ellerbeck, and the staff of Teachers College Press. Finally, but hardly least, I owe a special debt to Nel Noddings for tirelessly discussing with me the ideas in this book, for providing the foreword, and for years of caring support.

Introduction: Making Social Studies Matter

This book is about the teacher's role as curricular-instructional gatekeeper and its ramifications for social studies curriculum, instructional planning, teaching, and teacher education. As gate-keepers, teachers make the educational decisions in the place where they ultimately count: the classroom (Thornton, 1991). That is, they make the day-to-day decisions concerning both the subject matter and the experiences to which pupils have access and the nature of that subject matter and those experiences. *Gatekeeping* encompasses the decisions teachers make about curriculum and instruction and the criteria they use to make those decisions. Curricular decisions are defined as decisions about appropriate teaching goals and experiences to reach them. Instructional decisions concern how to teach within some explicit or implicit frame of reference (Shaver, 1979). Since teacher enactment of curriculum is inevitable, teachers ought to be prepared to do it well.

If educational-change efforts fail to alter how teachers view the purposes of their teaching, those efforts will flounder. Change in classrooms involves a process of mutual adaptation between the innovation and teachers (McLaughlin, 1997), but reformers have frequently disregarded this reality. Rather, they have relied on monocular prescriptions such as curriculum mandates, learning-objectives- or standards-driven instruction, competency-based teacher education, and different media of instruction such as movies and television or, more recently, computers. Characteristically, these approaches told practitioners what to do rather than educating them as gatekeepers. As a result, the history of social studies reform has often boiled down to change advocated but not realized (Hertzberg, 1981).

Change efforts must also eventually—if they haven't begun

with it—locate themselves in the now century-old debate about the field's proper content. This debate characteristically takes the form of disputes about relatively concrete issues such as what should be taught in American history or how many courses in state history should be required; however, usually underlying the surface of these disputes are deeper cleavages about what knowledge is of most worth and how it should be arranged for instruction or even the nature of knowledge itself (see Nelson, 2001).

At any rate, the core of school social studies programs has been, and continues to be, the social sciences, in which for purposes of brevity I include history and geography. In the schools, the mainstay social sciences are history, geography, and government (often in the guise of "civics"). Economics, sociology, anthropology, and psychology, in roughly that order of frequency, are sometimes present as well. The curriculum also contains less easily classifiable areas of social study (Dewey, 1969) such as current events. In other words, *social studies* is a curriculum term that includes the social sciences as well as other material. Although all the social sciences fall under the rubric of social studies, social studies includes content beyond the social science academic disciplines.

One further clarification seems necessary. "Social studies" and "*the* social studies" are sometimes used interchangeably, and to some extent I follow that convention. But occasionally—which I hope is apparent from the context—I refer to "the social studies" when I am trying to underscore that one social study such as history may function as a distinct course from another social study such as civics in the school curriculum.

Regardless of which version of social studies is adopted or what is named, it obviously contains an almost unbounded body of subject matter. Since not everything can be taught, it is scarcely surprising that different interest groups have championed different versions of social studies. Some educators recommend, for example, that we base the curriculum on material already gathered under the rubric of a discipline, material authoritatively endorsed as knowledge. Here, as Nel Noddings (1995) has pointed out, "the source of the material is considered more important than its likely usefulness in capturing students' interest" (p. 112). I refer to this view as a "social science" approach, what Basil Bernstein referred to as a "collection-type" curriculum (cited in

Hamilton, 1975)—for the most part social studies is taught as a collection of separate courses in individual social sciences such as geography or economics. An alternative conception is to see the curriculum as "ignoring disciplinary boundaries and organized around the needs of society, of students, or some combination thereof" (Hertzberg, 1981, p. 2; see also Thornton, 1994). I refer to this view as a "social education" approach. Although these two views can and do overlap, scarce time and energy ordinarily tilt the curriculum more in one direction than the other. Every social studies innovator eventually wrestles with finding a justifiable balance between these competing approaches to the curriculum. These differences about the curriculum's optimal form can be significant stumbling blocks to achieving consensus among interest groups in curriculum-reform efforts.

The passions expended on what the social studies curriculum should contain and how it should be organized have often been consuming for the field. Nonetheless, these definitional struggles, while far from trivial, may not always be as significant as has been widely assumed. Whatever *social studies* is taken to mean, its educational significance for students is primarily to be found in the enacted curriculum of classrooms. At this level, almost without regard to the kind of social studies program enacted, it seems that young people are dissatisfied. Viewed in this light, the struggles that have engaged generations of theorists seem less important. The same might be said for those who propose curriculum change as the remedy for young people not learning what they ought to learn in social studies. These critics seldom pause to consider that the unlearned material *has been taught* (Jenness, 1990, pp. 397–398), but young peoples' encounters with it leave many of them cold. While they may learn what is in the curriculum, they quickly forget it or fail to see its relationships to other subject matter. These disappointing experiences and outcomes suggest the need for a reexamination of the purposes driving both curriculum (and testing) policies and, in many cases, teacher gatekeeping.

Chronic controversy over the formal curriculum has also had another effect on the field: It has tended to obscure that, for all the disputes, there is consensus about several key features of social studies education. For instance, in spite of uncertainties about its proper name, what aims ought to be emphasized, and what form the curriculum should take, no responsible party seriously questions that social studies courses such as American history ought to be taught in American schools (Thornton, 2001c). So much so, in fact, that John Dewey (1966) warned of the two dominant social studies, geography and history: "Nowhere...is there is greater danger that subject matter will be accepted because it has become customary to teach and learn it" (p. 210).

Even figures otherwise as educationally as far apart as Dewey (1966) and Diane Ravitch or Lynne Cheney could probably find common ground in Dewey's case for the educational significance of social studies. Although the term *social studies* had yet to come into widespread use, Dewey had grasped the heart of its educational potential: "Geography and history," he wrote, "are the two great school resources for bringing about the enlargement of the significance of direct personal experience" (pp. 217–218). He concluded: "Thus our ordinary daily experiences cease to be things of the moment and gain enduring substance" (p. 209).

Social studies may be central to the educational process and, in broad terms at least, its educational significance agreed upon. However, it does *not* seem to matter to a significant proportion of young people. Although young people express higher interest in social studies topics than many topics from other school subjects, social studies as a subject is rated relatively low in interest among several curricular fields. The essence of the problem, John Goodlad (1984) believed, is that "the study topics become removed from their intrinsically human character" on their way to the social studies classroom (p. 212). He concluded: "It appears that we cannot assume the cultivation of goals most appropriate to the social sciences even when social studies courses appear in the curriculum" (p. 213). Of course, this problem is hardly new— as long ago as the late 19th century, the pioneer developmental psychologist G. Stanley Hall complained of history that "no subject so widely taught is, on the whole, taught so poorly" (cited in Saxe, 1991, p. 32).

What is relatively new is the realization by theorists, researchers, and policymakers of the salience of the teacher's gatekeeping role in educational reform. As Linda Darling-Hammond (1999) points out, for instance, teacher learning is now widely regarded as "a linchpin" of school reform. Of course, gatekeeping is important in all school subjects; however, it may be especially important in social studies. Whereas the proper subject matters of school algebra courses are relatively circumscribed, for instance, the proper scope and sequence of social studies is less apparent. It can, and frequently does, degenerate into a flood of information. Moreover, teacher preference for classroom order over academic engagement may further undermine the coherence of subject matter, resulting in student obfuscation, indifference, or both (McNeil, 1986). In other words, even standards-driven and test-prodded curriculum fails to dictate how a topic such as the Emancipation Proclamation should be approached (see Grant, 2003). Should earlier attempts at emancipation be stressed? Or its constitutional dubiousness? Or its role as a historic turning point? At the level of a classroom instructional program, even a strictly prescribed curriculum can neither wholly arrange itself nor teach itself.

Teachers may tend the gate well or poorly, consciously or unconsciously, but their gatekeeping is unavoidable. Unless teacher gatekeeping changes, the curricular-instructional status quo, which seems to please almost nobody, will remain impervious to fundamental change. Such change requires a comprehensive approach to educating teachers to be gatekeepers; we must look at the major elements of gatekeeping and their interconnections as one element is interrelated with the rest. Thus educating gatekeepers is not just isolated attempts at improving, say, subject matter knowledge or gaining greater facility in leading classroom discussion. Rather, it requires simultaneous attention to both curriculum and method and their interrelationships. In an important sense, method and curriculum merge as the way that content is taught and the classroom milieu more generally become part of the content learned and vice versa (Eisner, 1982).

This book brings together the major elements of curricular-instructional gatekeeping. More specifically, I present a basis for preparing purposeful teachers in curriculum and instruction. Although I hope that educators at all levels will find this useful, this book is more an exercise in the theory of curriculum, instruction, and teacher education than a methods manual telling the reader "how to do it" step by step. It is aimed at expanding educational imagination so that other educators can apply the ideas developed herein for the necessarily specific circumstances of their locales.

Understandably, practitioners—by whom I mean social studies teachers, supervisors, administrators, curriculum materials developers, state and local curriculum agencies, providers of pre- and in-service education, and others—may be less interested in theoretical matters than in practical results. But given that quick and easy remedies have repeatedly failed to solve the problems of social studies gatekeeping, I hope readers will be more inclined to accept my premise that it is imperative to develop purposeful teachers if we are truly interested in educational improvement. In this scheme, for instance, deep understanding and facility with curriculum becomes not something reserved for later graduate work but an indispensable part of educating even beginning teachers (Zumwalt, 1989). Curriculum, in other words, is not merely a product developed by distal "experts" as a script for teachers, but a classroom enactment, properly differing from one classroom to the next. The "same" curriculum can be arranged and taught in countless ways (Connelly & Ben-Peretz, 1997; Thornton, 1988).

Sound gatekeeping requires consideration of educational purposes, a task some practitioners prefer to avoid. They may judge aims talk as unnecessary, and they may even resist it—their job, they might say, is to deliver instruction. Such a view, however, is logically untenable. The choice is not whether teachers will make decisions about purposes, but how. As a former president of the National Council for the Social Studies pointedly observed, avoidance of aims talk is less mischievous than "mindless" (Shaver, 1977). Lack of considered purpose does not necessarily lead to poor practice, but it does commonly lead to indifferent practice, where instruction lacks an adequate compass to guide what is worth teaching at a given time to a given group of students. In these circumstances, Dewey (1991a) warned, "the supposed end for which [social studies] were introduced—the development of more intelligent citizenship in all the ranges of citizenship...will be missed" (p. 185). It seems to be the realization of this danger—of the "end" being "missed"—that apparently persuades so many youngsters that social studies does not matter (Thornton, 2001d).

The remainder of this book is divided into two main parts. The first part lays a theoretical foundation for the second part, in which I attempt to provide a principled basis for curriculum development, instructional planning, teaching methods, and teacher education. Rather than approaching theory and practice as being dichotomous,

I proceed on the assumption that they are mutually dependent and informative: "Theory is practice become conscious of itself, and practice is realized theory" (cited in Marsden, 1995, p. 1).

In Chapter 1, I examine two views of social studies, which overlap in some respects but are still distinguishable. They have been the subject of chronic debate: Is social studies properly understood to denote the study of a federation of the individual social sciences or an integrated field, which draws on relevant social science, organized around the needs of society, students, or both? Particular scrutiny is given to the relative weight that should be assigned in explaining whether the formal view of curriculum adopted—that is, the social sciences as separate subjects (with possibly some attention to material not drawn from the academic disciplines such as current events) or a more integrated social education program—or teacher gatekeeping has the more significant effect on the curriculum enacted in the classroom.

In Chapter 2 we switch from curriculum theory and its possible effects in the classroom to more historical concerns. I focus on how the curriculum has actually been organized over the past century. In particular, I examine two archetypes of the social science and social education views, the survey course in American history and the Problems of Democracy course, respectively. I argue that a social science view has been more associated with prespecified bodies of disciplinary knowledge, while a social education view tends to present greater possibilities for identifying relevant bodies of knowledge during instruction.

Rounding out this first part of the book, in Chapter 3 I analyze the conventional sources of social studies aims. As the historian Charles A. Beard (1932) memorably put it, "Instruction in social studies in the schools is conditioned by the spirit and letter of scholarship, by the realities and ideas of the society in which it is carried on, and by the nature and limitations of the teaching and learning process" (p. 2). Since the chief problem of school social studies programs is frequently an overreliance on the transmission of information and disconnected skills, a more purposeful approach to gatekeeping is needed in many cases. Teachers, as noted, frequently eschew aims talk as somebody else's business—their job is to enact a curriculum developed by outside authorities in the classroom on a day-to-day basis. An important result of this belief is disconnection between the aims that are supposed to animate instruction in the first place and the purposes pursued in classrooms. In this chapter I present illustrations of the kinds of deliberation in which teachers need to engage if this state of affairs is to change.

In the second part of the book we explore the ramifications of the preceding part for practice. In Chapter 4, I discuss how purposes inform curriculum development. Here, and in subsequent chapters, special attention is devoted to the role of the classroom teacher in educational planning. In particular, I argue that a sound curriculum derives more specific goals from broad aims. I contend that curriculum work is the most intellectual work of teaching, albeit intellectual in a somewhat different way from that of the academy. It can be one of the greatest sources of professional satisfaction for teachers. Indeed, it may be salient in what keeps talented teachers in the classroom.

Chapter 5 is about methods of instruction. Possibly no part of this book is more important than this chapter, as method seems to be at the heart of what ails social studies. Unfortunately, too frequently these days method is reduced to a series of procedures, to an essentially technical undertaking. Method, however, is always both normative and procedural—no technique can be value neutral, nor can an educational purpose be actualized without some procedure. Thus, the selection of effective methods is a cornerstone of purposeful teaching. Although space prohibits consideration of the entire range of possible methods, selected methods and social studies instantiations are presented.

Given the foregoing demands of gatekeeping, Chapter 6 takes up how we should prepare teachers. This is possibly the least conventional section of the book, as I argue that American teacher education programs are poorly aligned with the demands of gatekeeping and need thorough rethinking (Thornton, 2001a). It seems unlikely that we can add still more to already overburdened teacher education programs, and, in any case, more of the same probably won't help much. Rather, we need to rethink the kinds of subject matter that teachers need and how this can better be aligned with professional coursework, especially the methods course. Rejecting an all-or-nothing approach, I suggest that many of my ideas can be implemented in teacher education programs as they currently exist.

Finally, in Chapter 7 I present a brief afterword exploring the implications of gatekeeping given the prevailing realities of schooling in the contemporary United States. There is now at least some empirical evidence (e.g., Hess, 2002; Stigler & Hiebert, 1999) to add to the intuitive belief that gatekeeping can be systematically improved through innovative teacher education. The process of educating gatekeepers offers, of course, no quick fixes, but there seems no alternative if the pendulum of reform advocated/reform abandoned that goes nowhere is to be broken.

1 Why Gatekeeping Matters More Than Curriculum Change

It is sometimes pointed out, with either humor or derision, that social studies educators have spent a century arguing over what the field "is" and never reached consensus. Certainly these arguments have been a dominant theme in the theoretical social studies literature. Specifically, should *social studies* simply denote a collective noun for the social sciences such as history, geography, government, economics, sociology, and anthropology; or should it mean an integration of subject matter from those subjects and related material? While theorists have argued back and forth over this question for a century, practitioners seldom express great interest in it. It is widely recognized that this gulf between theorist and practitioner is a formidable obstacle to curricular-instructional change. But what is less remarked upon may be more significant: Gatekeeping seems more crucial to curriculum and instruction than the form the curriculum takes.

In this chapter we consider this perennial battle over whether social studies should be an aggregation of the social sciences or an integration of them. More particularly, I argue that while social studies educators may have overrated the significance of which form the curriculum takes, they may correspondingly have underrated the significance of teachers' curricular-instructional gatekeeping. As Jere Brophy and his colleagues (Brophy, Prawat, & McMahon, 1991) have concluded:

> It appears that the effectiveness of a social studies curriculum for developing students' understanding of and ability to apply its content depends less on what general topics are covered than on what content is selected, how that content is organized and presented to students and developed through discourse and activities, and how learning is assessed through assignments and tests. (p. 187)

Whichever curriculum form is adopted, teacher gatekeeping implies that there are almost as many educational possibilities *within* an integrated social-education view or a social-science-as-separate-subjects view as there are *between* them (see Jenness, 1990, pp. 296–297). In other words, prior to and during its classroom enactment, teachers have great leeway to interpret a prescribed curriculum. A curriculum offers a series of "potentials," not a straitjacket that dictates what a curriculum "means" (Ben-Peretz, 1975).

In this chapter I first trace the boundaries of persistent debate over the proper definition of *social studies,* or whatever title is selected for that part of the school curriculum that deals with the study of society. I suggest that the role of teacher curricular-instructional gatekeeping is crucial in three important elements of the educational process: (1) aims, (2) subject matter and instructional methods, and (3) student interest and effort. Is gatekeeping, which blends curriculum and instruction, more educationally significant than whether the curriculum adheres to an aggregation or integrated model?

DEFINING SOCIAL STUDIES

The widespread replacement of the 19th-century term *history and allied subjects* by *social studies* occurred in the 1910s and 1920s. This change has customarily been accorded great significance; however, it may not be as consequential as has been assumed, because it failed to settle the form the social studies ought to take in school programs. In other words, *social studies* turned out to be a term as open to varying interpretations as the *history and allied subjects* it replaced. In this sense, the National Council for the Social Studies (NCSS), founded in 1921, had an ambiguous charge from the outset. It could be understood to be merely a clearinghouse for the dissemination of new ideas and materials to inform treatment of the individual social sciences in school programs or it could be understood as underwriting a new, integrated field of study. NCSS's founders disagreed on which alternative (Thornton, 1996) was correct.

The case of two leading NCSS pioneers illustrates this contested meaning of social studies. Edgar Dawson, NCSS's first secretary, received complaints that social studies as an integrated field was threatening school courses in the separate social sciences. Dawson stoutly denied that NCSS stood for an integrated conception of social studies:

> The use by the National Council of the term "social studies" did not arise from any prejudice in favor of a hash of all kinds of subject matter thrown together....The term...was adopted as the only one now available that distinguishes the social studies from other parts of the school curriculum (cited in Vanaria, 1958, p. 91).

Dawson's attachment to the social science approach contrasted with the view of Harold Rugg, another social studies pioneer. Rugg (1936) regarded the individual social sciences as hopelessly ill equipped for the task of educating students for life. "Nothing short of genius on the part of a student," he declared, "could create an ordered understanding of modern life from such a compartmentalized arrangement of material" (p. 332).

This division has endured. Although the terms of debate have varied over the decades, the basic issue has been essentially the same. Social science champions have charged that social education is a mishmash of information and skills, lacking in substance, and insufficiently attuned to the concerns and methods of the traditional academic subjects. In this view social studies is taken to be synonymous with social education and stands condemned as "social stew," an inferior but dangerous curricular rival for the social sciences, especially in the eyes of historians (Bestor, 1953; Nevins, 1942; Wilentz, 1997).

Since the 1980s, advocates of an almost exclusively social science approach to the social studies curriculum have been unrelentingly critical of social education (e.g., Egan, 1999; Ravitch, 1989). Critics have attacked social education even at the elementary level, where it is unclear how the subjects we teach are or should be related to the academic disciplines (see Sosniak, 1999, pp. 190–191). The critics have particularly targeted the integrated expanding-environments sequence of the elementary schools, which moves outward from the familiar notions of family, neighborhood, and community in the primary grades of kindergarten through the third grade to state, regions, nation, Western Hemisphere, and world in the upper elementary grades, 4 through 6. Diane Ravitch (1987) bluntly dismissed the primary-grades portion of expanding environments as "tot sociology," alleging it is a hodgepodge of trivial material children already know, such as how their local community functions.

In contrast, defenders of expanding environments in the primary grades have noted that although children may be familiar with concepts such as shelter, they are unable to explain why, say, different kinds of shelter might be used in different kinds of physical environments (Brophy & Alleman, 2000). More generally, expanding environments has been defended as being based on a "psychological" rather than a "logical" arrangement of subject matter, thus making the material more learnable (see Thornton, 2001c), and as providing a richer and more useful view of the social sciences, since students experience the subject matter in a broad, meaningful context (Muessig, 1987). The well-known progressive educator Lucy Sprague Mitchell (1991) demonstrated through geography that even programs in an individual social science were effective when they utilized a kind of subject matter organization comparable to that of expanding environments.

In place of expanding environments, critics have urged using material in the primary grades that is distant in time and space, rich in stories of the exotic. This material, its own potpourri, would be derived primarily from history, geography, and biographical and mythical stories. In the upper-clementary grades, the critics suggest courses more clearly distinguishable as individual social sciences.

In contrast to the critics, other educators have expressed fears that a primary-grades curriculum that stresses subject matters such as myths, tall tales, and exotic locales may compromise or sacrifice the goals of social education in favor of literacy goals (Alleman & Brophy, 1993a; Dewey, 1990, pp. 154–155). Moreover, social educators have pointed out that in the upper grades of the elementary school, there is nothing inherent in the social sciences that prepare youngsters for contemporary life. Indeed, there is a danger that courses in the social sciences too easily devolve into knowledge transmission, at the expense of life relevance (Engle & Ochoa, 1988; Rugg, 1921, 1936). It was in this spirit that Edgar Wesley (1967), after a lifetime of leadership in the teaching of history, urged the abolition of history courses because there is no mandate for the memorization of historical information. History, he argued, was still an indispensable part of the curriculum, but it should be used as repository of information, rather like a dictionary, for addressing issues that matter in the contemporary world.

As may be apparent, the social education model never took as strong a hold in secondary education as in elementary education.

The cliché that elementary schools teach the child and secondary schools the subject is exaggerated but not entirely inaccurate. In secondary education, most social studies courses are in a particular social science such as economics, government, history, or geography. More integrated courses in secondary schools tend to be tepid forms of integration such as the combination of world history and geography, with the sum being called "global studies." The great exception is the archetypal integrated social studies course at the secondary level, Problems of Democracy (POD). Although less widely taught in recent decades, from the 1920s to the 1960s it seems to have enrolled more students than did any other secondary social studies course apart from American history (Singleton, 1980).

POD was initially conceived as a way to combine material from government, economics, and sociology and apply it to the study of contemporary societal problems. As will be discussed in Chapter 2, however, it seems questionable whether the course in most places was truly integrative, as had been originally intended; teachers and the entrenched culture of high schools (and to a lesser extent middle schools) tend to be respecters of the boundaries of each social science. Advocates of POD and civics, therefore, want to ensure that these courses do not become watered-down versions of college courses in government rather than being an effective integration of material directed at how society and government actually function (Dewey, 1991a; Oliver & Shaver, 1966; Parker, 2003, pp. 110–121).

The struggle for curricular supremacy between social education and the social sciences seems to have been significantly affected by the standards movement and its associated high-stakes tests, which emerged in the 1990s. At the national level, unprecedented weight was given to the social science model. The federal government funded standards in the traditional social sciences, blithely ignoring more integrated views of social studies. The prototypical social-science standards were in history, in which there seems to have been no more than a token effort at developing educational criteria to justify content selection. Rather, the apparent criterion guiding content selection in the national history standards was the then current academic interests of the historians who participated in creating the standards. Although the history standards contained assertions that the material identified would advance important educational aims such as good citizenship, no convincing case was made about how or why. In their inattention to a range of both social science and social education aims, the history national standards were more narrowly academic in their conception than the recommendations of practically all significant reports issued by social science groups, education groups, or both since the birth of the modern curriculum at the close of the 19th century.

In contrast to the case of the social sciences, no federal dollars went into making social studies standards. NCSS nonetheless launched its own modestly funded standards-making effort. This resulted in 10 themes that blended the concerns of social scientists with other criteria such as the education of citizens (NCSS, 1994). Perhaps partially conforming to the spirit of the social science standards, NCSS gave the social sciences greater weight than was customary in previous NCSS curriculum position statements. The NCSS standards pleased neither strong proponents of separate standards in each of the social sciences nor strong advocates of social education.

Although there has been debate and understandable confusion over whether states and localities should adhere to either the social science or the social studies standards, the differences between the two approaches seem overstated. Both approaches, for example, pay homage to the social sciences and both assert the life relevance of these traditional academic subjects. Moreover, both sets of standards put great store in the boundaries, content, and methods of each social science. While this is scarcely surprising with standards in the social sciences, it is less evident why these disciplinary strictures should be given such weight in social studies standards. Indeed, the social studies standards, notwithstanding their thematic organization, are to a considerable extent organized around the social sciences also. For instance, Standard 3, "people, places, and environments," seems to boil down to geography, while Theme 7, "production, distribution, and consumption," seems to boil down to economics.

The two approaches to standards also exhibit other similarities. For example, the grades 5–12 U.S. history standards claim their relevance to citizenship education thus: "[Without historical knowledge] we cannot achieve the informed, discriminating citizenship essential to effective participation in the democratic processes of government" (National Center for History in the Schools, 1995, p. 1). The language of the social studies standards on this same issue is quite similar: "The vitality of a democracy depends upon the education and participation of its citizens" (NCSS, 1994, p. vii). Furthermore, both the history and the social studies standards, critics charge, minimize the treatment of controversial issues, skills such as critical thinking that are essential for citizenship, and civic participation (Ochoa-Becker, 2001).

It is also apparent that both the history standards and the social studies standards give short shrift to gatekeeping concerns. They appear to share optimism largely unwarranted by the history of curricular-instructional change that curriculum mandates will, more or less, lead to corresponding changes in the curriculum enacted in classrooms. To be sure, both documents exhort imaginative methods in teaching curricula based on their standards, but similar exhortations in the past have seldom effectively influenced how the curricular-instructional gate is tended (Cuban, 1991). Curricular-instructional business-as-usual, whatever the content, frequently fails to productively engage students (Thornton, 2001d).

While neither an integrated social-education model nor a social-science-as-a-separate-subject model has entirely prevailed, this inconclusive outcome fails to dim the optimism of the forecasts that supporters of each model regularly claim would result if their version were fully and effectively embraced. Perhaps the allure of curriculum change is that it will carry all else with it. But as noted, the historical record fails to sustain this happy picture. Whichever view of curricular organization is adopted, gatekeeping seems to suffer from much the same problems. In this regard, a lesson learned from the implementation of the New Social Studies curricula that were developed in the 1960s is instructive: Curriculum change fails to occur when it is out of step with teachers' gatekeeping (see Shaver, 1997). Tried-and-true practices—even if they seem less than ideal to outside observers—persist. In the aftermath of the failure of most teachers to adopt the well-funded, ambitious curricular-instructional approaches of the New Social Studies, researchers grasped a basic element of why gatekeeping has proved so hard to change: Teachers who failed to adopt new social studies materials "are generally not obstructionists." Instead, it is simply more appropriate to them to continue doing what they have done before—practices consistent with their own values and beliefs and those they perceive, probably accurately, to be those of their communities. The new materials just don't "fit" (Shaver, Davis, & Helburn, p. 12, 1980). Comprehensive reform is a tall order, and perhaps, as I argue below, reformers should set more modest and realizable goals.

Thus far I have argued that educators have devoted much attention to the model to which social studies should adhere. Should social studies be an aggregation of some or all of the social sciences, possibly mimicking the "adult" subjects? Or should social studies be an integrated field in which scholarship serves as but one of several criteria to select content?

In either case, however, the model adopted may fail to have beneficial effects on instructional arrangements without more attention to gatekeeping than has been customary in educational-change efforts in the social studies. A particular problem has been the apparently ineffective line of communication between designers of social studies innovations and the concerns of teachers as gatekeepers. Whether teachers willingly open the gate, partially open the gate, are unable to open the gate, and so on clearly matters. As I suggest in the following section, why, when, for whom, and how teachers open the curricular-instructional gate points to the centrality of purpose to effective teaching (see Barton & Levstik, 2004, pp. 254–261). Educational purposes do not always, however, have a one-to-one correspondence to the problems and possibilities presented by either the social science model or the social education model.

AIMS TALK

The significance afforded the social science–social education dispute would appear to denote widely disparate educational aims. This, too, may be less clear-cut than heated rhetoric frequently suggests. Consider, for instance, an aim much at the forefront of American educational policy in recent decades, that of "cultural literacy." It is frequently invoked as a justification for a social science approach to social studies. Unless distinct social sciences—with history, geography, and government generally afforded most prominence—are studied, so the argument goes, young people will "miss" vital knowledge that is necessary for communication in the common culture (e.g., Hirsch, 1987). Secretary of Education William Bennett (1987) put it this way:

We want our students—whatever their plans for the future—to take from high school a shared body of knowledge and skills, a common language of ideas, a common moral and intellectual discipline....A broad, deep, and effective core curriculum is possible for almost all American secondary school students. (p. 4)

Adherents of this view customarily draw unflattering portraits of social education as a wishy-washy alternative. Social educators have responded by arguing that:

Knowledge attainment is not a sufficiently broad purpose to guide program development or to inspire modern students....The prospect of learning something new may inspire some of us, but for most [people], knowledge is merely a means to some larger end. (Cassidy & Kurfman, 1977, p. 2)

Moreover, they are skeptical that standardization of the curriculum will necessarily deliver either cognitive or affective improvements in many circumstances. Wayne Ross (1997) has observed of curriculum standardization:

The primary tension, today and historically, in curriculum reform efforts is between centralized and grassroots decision-making....Operationally, curriculum standards projects in social studies are antidemocratic because they severely restrict the legitimate role of teachers and other educational professionals as well as the public in participating in the conversation about the origin, nature, and ethics of knowledge taught in the social studies curriculum. (p. 15)

Although there are clear differences between the cultural literacy, which is one variant of the social science model, and social education positions, it may be important to also notice some significant commonalties. As is evident in their references to a common culture and "larger ends," both rely on arguments that extend beyond knowledge "for its own sake" to what ordinary people need in order to prosper in everyday life. That is, they both speak to the demands of general education. It may be that much of the supposed dichotomy between social science and social education approaches results from a failure to engage in satisfactory aims talk. Moreover, is there any good reason to believe that teachers, as gatekeepers, consider either knowledge aims or life-relevance aims unimportant? Shallow consideration of curriculum aims and teacher gatekeeping may have created an unnecessary dichotomy between scholarly aims and life-relevance aims.

Gatekeeping has tended, of course, to be shunted aside since the ascendancy of the strong movement of the past two decades that is devoted mainly to increasing the share of the curriculum assigned to history and geography as separate subjects (Thornton, 1990). This movement, which has often taken culturally conservative form, has strongly castigated the allegedly "presentist" aim of integrated social education programs. Solid academic aims have been contrasted with allegedly wispy social studies aims.

But the underlying aims talk of conservatives, or the lack thereof, regarding all this has been insufficiently examined. For example, conservatives have decried aims other than academic ones and appear to accept as self-evident that the only aim worth pursuing is an academic curriculum, based on an agreed-upon common body of knowledge that prepares all students, regardless of their goals, for college.

Ravitch (1989) contends, for instance, that a college-preparatory curriculum for all was once the agreed aim in U.S. education. She says the 1890s were a period when sage educational reformers endorsed a social science perspective and on that basis devised a rigorous, one-size-fits-all college-preparation curriculum in "history and allied subjects." Unfortunately, in her eyes, later progressive reformers introduced "vulgar utilitarianism"—less substantive, social education courses in which the autonomy of history was breached, courses designed to be relevant to modern living (p. 68) and taught by deficient gatekeepers (p. 57). Leaving aside for now that history and allied subjects was itself justified by appeals to civic relevance, how seriously should we take claims that integrationist social studies displaced substantive and distinct courses in the social sciences?

Unlike at the beginning of the 21st century, serious aims talk was a conspicuous feature of the 1890s, the decade in which the modern American curriculum was born. Two 1890s committees are customarily deemed particularly significant in legitimating history and allied subjects as cornerstones of the emerging modern curriculum. The first committee, convened by the National Education Association (NEA), issued its report on secondary-school subjects in 1893 (NEA, 1893). The NEA convened the conference because in the 1880s burgeoning public high schools had for the first time overtaken private academies as the dominant institutions of secondary education. The proper aims of a rapidly developing public-education sector were thus a matter of some urgency.

Aims talk in the 1890s, however, can only be understood within the context of a broader transformation of thinking that was overtaking American education. The image of the developing child was changing, for example, from that of a passive receptacle of information to that of an active meaning-maker. The teacher's main role had been as drillmaster. But this new image of the child required, among other things, a rethinking of teaching methods. Nineteenth-century teaching had focused on students' learning material by rote. If, however, young people were to learn to think and solve problems for themselves, teachers needed to be organizers of learning opportunities rather than mere information dispensers.

This transformation in the aims of education was evident in the social-subjects component of the NEA report, composed by the so-called Committee of Ten. It marks a transition from 19th- to 20th-century educational thought (albeit a transition not entirely complete by 1893). Ravitch and others, however, have zeroed in on one aim of the Ten's report: that high school instruction in history and related subjects ought to be the same for pupils on their way to college as for the noncollege bound (NEA, 1893). Ravitch is correct that the Ten wanted to ensure that the noncollege bound did not receive an impoverished curriculum; however, she takes this one point out of context.

The Ten's main concern was to identify a course of study and associated teaching methods that were appropriate for general education. This was necessary if history and allied subjects were to become standard components of the curriculum then taking shape—only a small percentage of American youth attended high school in the 1890s, but this was (rightly as it turned out) expected to grow rapidly. Thus, the Ten went to great lengths to justify why history was as educationally significant as curricular rivals such as language, natural science, and mathematics. To this end, the Ten were eclectic in the aims they embraced. They invoked moribund faculty psychology, for example, to argue that history had unique potential for training the mind in judgment (pp. 168–169). They also embraced other rationales that were then growing in popularity. For instance, they claimed that history helped to develop better citizens, provided moral training, and could be applied to current events (pp. 169–170). In addition, they considered how history should be related to its allied subjects. For instance, they suggested that civil government should be integrated with the American history course. In other words, the Ten's recommendations of one track for all by no means justifies Ravitch's claim that this was a blanket endorsement for a social science approach unfettered by anything else but the academic demands of a college-preparation curriculum.

Several years after the Ten, the American Historical Association (AHA) established a Committee of Seven, which also considered the aims of history and allied subjects (AHA, 1899). Its recommendations were similar to the Ten's and its adoption rate in the schools surpassed that of the Ten (Hertzberg, 1981, p. 16). As had the Ten, the Seven provided a rationale for history that extended beyond the academic to general education. The Seven (AHA, 1899) concluded that:

> The student who is...led to look at matters historically, has some mental equipment for a comprehension of the political and social problems that will confront him in everyday life, and has received practical preparation for social adaptation and for forceful participation in civic activities. (p. 18)

The 1890s reformers, then, favored a range of aims, some not strictly academic, for history and allied subjects. Moreover, those aims share significant similarities with those adopted by later reformers of whom Ravitch disapproves. As Linda Levstik (1996) noted in the case of history, struggles over whether history should be taught "as a feature of cross-disciplinary citizenship education" versus as "a separate discipline 'for its own sake'...has been a specious argument" as advocates of history for its own sake also make citizenship claims for it (p. 23). The sharp break Ravitch detects between the 1890s reports and NEA's Committee on Social Studies 2 decades later is surely exaggerated and, perhaps, not even a break at all.

Critics have portrayed NEA's 1916 Committee on Social Studies (NEA, 1994) report as the main villain, as a sharp turn from the aims of the 1890s reports. Although the 1916 report suggests that the topics in the curriculum ought to come from the students' present life interests, which the Ten, for instance, did not mention, the social sciences are scarcely ignored (Watras, 2002). The evident obligation felt by the 1916 committee to justify *what* social science subject matter should be taught hardly means that they repudiated the worth of the social sciences or the earlier reports. Rather, the 1916 Committee on Social Studies (NEA, 1994) believed that the aims of education were broader than the scope of the social sciences collectively, and certainly of any one of the social sciences individually. Since they believed that these aims should drive the selection of subject matter, they more forcefully underscored than the 1890s committees that social science knowledge is not an end in itself in general education: "Whatever their value from the point of view of personal culture," the social studies "should have for their conscious and constant purpose the cultivation of good citizenship" (p. 9).

Rather than abandoning scholarship, the Committee on Social Studies was marching in step with social science scholarship by wanting to put scholarly knowledge to use in society. In this respect, they paralleled developments in the academic disciplines such as history. The "new" history of the Progressive Era was aimed at identifying the roots of current social problems. Instead of a break from the Ten and the Seven, the Committee on Social Studies' report "represented growth and development within the field" (Whelan, 1991, p. 200).

Nevertheless the false dichotomy between what was allegedly said by the the 1890s committees and the 1916 committee has persisted to the present day at the level of policy and theory. But perhaps in more tangible matters than aims, such as subject matter and methods, the social science and social education approaches actually are at odds. This will be considered in the following section.

SUBJECT MATTER AND METHODS

Whether named history and allied subjects or social studies, social sciences such as history, geography, and government have been a standard part of the curriculum since at least the 1890s. Did the change from history and allied subjects to social studies, as critics have complained, bring about significant changes in subject matter and methods?

In terms of subject matter, if we compare the course recommendations of the Ten of 1893 and the Committee on Social Studies of 1916, there are differences, but on close inspection they are not great. Both the Ten and the 1916 committee recommended a central place for history. The latter committee did rearrange some subject matters; but in both reports, civics in some form, geography, and political economy were featured, whether they appeared under different course names or were integrated with history courses. For example, civics and political economy appeared in courses the Ten labeled history, and history appeared in courses the Committee on Social Studies called geography and civics (Watras, 2004). Similarly the Ten (NEA, 1893) endorsed methods "drawn from the experience of the community" (p. 197), while the 1916 committee emphasized community civics.

Course titles may, however, still conceal significant differences about teaching methods. More clearly than the 1890s reports, for instance, the 1916 report calls for methods that tie subject matter directly to students' everyday lives. It nevertheless seems questionable whether the rearrangement of courses and their sequence that the 1916 report brought about led to equally significant changes in teaching methods. Although the historical evidence is fragmentary, most of it points more to continuity than to change in methods (Cuban, 1991; Evans, 2004). Prominent educators of the period seem to concur. For example, as noted, Rugg (1936) was still complaining in the 1930s that methods suitable for the social sciences were too frequently substituted for methods suitable for social education.

Dewey possibly provides an even better indicator of the extent to which change occurred, as he had urged fundamental changes in method since the 1890s. Whether courses were labeled as social sciences, for example, geography and history, or as social studies, Dewey argued that methods should be suitable for social education. He seems to have doubted, however, that name changes altered much that was significant about methods commonly used. In *Democracy and Education,* first published in 1916, Dewey (1966) devoted a chapter to the significance of geography and history. He warned that unless the methods used involved "penetration" of information (p. 210), the subjects would fail to contribute to a "socialized intelligence," which informs contemporary civic life (p. 217).

Two decades later, Dewey (1991a) was speaking about "the social studies," among them geography and history; however, his message about method, the arrangement of subject matter in use, was unchanged. He advocated the same penetration of information if worthwhile social education were to take place. "The crucial question," Dewey wrote, "is the extent to which the material of the social studies, whether economics or politics or history or sociology, whatever it may be, is taught simply as information about present society or is taught in connection with things that are done, that need to be done, and how to do them" (p. 185).

The evidence, then, seems to suggest that changing names, from *history and allied subjects* to *social studies,* did not necessarily result in significant changes in gatekeeping regarding subject matter or method. It may be worth examining one final area where perhaps the formal organization of the curriculum outweighs the importance of gatekeeping: student engagement with the curriculum.

STUDENT INTEREST AND EFFORT

Wise educators have long recognized that interest and effort in education are intertwined. The most obvious reason for students' lack of effort in social studies is that it fails to interest them. The obverse seems to be the case also. That is, students may expend effort but have no real interest in the material. Denise Pope (2001) calls this "doing school," a situation in which academically "successful" students lack intrinsic interest in their studies but are academically accomplished. These young people have learned how much effort is necessary to expend for what extrinsic reward. What is learned in doing school has few deep effects (at least educative ones), and the subject matter is rapidly forgotten.

Building genuine student interest in work—surely the best route to student engagement and achievement—is a challenge for both "successful" and less successful students. Recognizing the educational importance of this challenge, Alfred North Whitehead (1929) observed:

> There can be no mental development without interest. Interest is the *sine qua non* for attention and apprehension. You may endeavour to excite interest by means of birch rods, or you may coax it by the incitement of pleasurable activity. But without interest there will be no progress. Now the natural mode by which living organisms are excited towards suitable self-development is enjoyment. (p. 48)

But is there any compelling reason to believe that one way of formal organization of a curriculum in and of itself guarantees the generation of greater student interest?

Since interest is generated by enjoyment, this suggests finding consonant material and methods. Often this is presented as an issue of motivation, and a great deal of time and energy is put into "motivating" students. But thoughtful observers doubt that interest can be entirely externally generated. As Dewey (1975) noted, it is a mistake to look *"for* a motive for the study or the lesson, instead of a motive *in* it" (p. 61). Efforts to coerce "motivation" are unlikely to work if we are interested in more than ritualistic doing school.

None of this is to say that young people cannot be motivated; but motivation that does not rely entirely on extrinsic reward must involve students having some say in formulating the purposes of what they study (Alleman & Brophy, 1993b; Dewey, 1963; Stodolsky et al., 1991). This seems to suggest that the curriculum must be individualized to some extent and, thus, is more consistent with a curriculum that to a considerable degree emerges out of classroom interactions than with one that is entirely pre-planned. Even more important, teachers in this scheme would need to have latitude in their gatekeeping to address the purposes of their students. Even when learning or content standards weigh heavily on the curricular-instructional gate, teachers in just about any course ought to have some flexibility and give their students at least some choice in what they study. For example, in a geography unit on Mexico, one activity might be a project for which individual students select for in-depth examination a topic reflective of their interest—such as from music, architecture, or sports or regarding gender roles.

Seen from this perspective, prescriptive standards in the social sciences such as those adopted in the 1990s reinforce the tendency for social studies courses to ignore student interests. Perhaps more interactive social education courses, such as New York State's Participation in Government course, provide greater opportunities for tapping student interests (although such courses are the least likely to have attached high-stakes tests and hence are of low status). Strong critics of the social science approach go further, suggesting that the traditional academic subjects have far too remote a connection to the interests of pupils. Nel Noddings (2002a), for example, contends that the stranglehold of traditional academic subjects on the school curriculum must be broken if we are serious about pursuing student interests. All students, she says, are interested in what makes friends, good neighbors, and harmonious family members and are willing to discuss perennial existential questions about birth, death, love, and so on (pp. 136–141). Noddings would use the material of the social sciences to address these vital questions of human existence, but "a complete reconstruction" of social studies should begin with the needs of students, not with the social sciences (p. 114).

Adherents of the traditional academic subjects insist, of course, that *properly taught,* the social sciences would capture the interest of students. But should we suspect that this may sometimes be a cop-out? Certainly we can point to examples of high student engagement with this kind of academic material; however, looking beneath the surface of such cases may reveal more than properly taught social science and a good deal of relating it to the life interests of the students (see Flinders, 1996). Perhaps we should ask, as in the 1970s, that when social science courses are required (versus given as electives for the deeply interested) for students, some attempt be made to make it relevant to young people (see Kownslar, 1974b).

In this chapter I have suggested that gatekeeping plays a significant part in shaping the meaning of the social studies curriculum, whatever else may be involved. I have also demonstrated that normative questions (what ought to be done) and procedural questions (how it is to be accomplished) are intertwined. Thus, educational judgments are unavoidable in gatekeeping and, as I shall develop more fully later, desirable. Moreover, since educational judgments must be made, it is surely disingenuous (and sometimes, one can't help but suspect, self-serving) to pretend an argument can be made for the role of a social science in general education without resort, perhaps tacitly or even unconsciously, to educational criteria. What is taught of, for example, history, in school programs is a subset of historical knowledge. Its selection is an *educational,* not a *historical,* decision. As the distinguished geographer Isaiah Bowman (1934) once pointed out, "The logic that leads to a discovery of new truth is not the logic that provides system to a given body of truths intended to facilitate learning about them" (p. 217). How does that "system" play out in archetypes of the social science and social education approaches to social studies?

2 How Has the Social Studies Curriculum Been Organized?

Something recognizably akin to the contemporary social studies curriculum began to emerge near the close of the 19th century. Even then, however, tension existed about whether this curriculum should foreground the social sciences or social education. In this chapter I examine how archetypes of the social science and social education perspectives developed and appraise how they fared in practice. I argue that where the curriculum maker begins—with questions about what scholars suggest is most worth teaching from the social sciences or what knowledge is most relevant to the individual and social demands of contemporary living—ordinarily shapes the kind of educational program that emerges. Nevertheless, both the social science and social education approaches end up in practice facing similar obstacles and possibilities, resulting in a greater similarity in school programs than their theoretical rationales might suggest.

EMERGENCE OF SOCIAL STUDIES AS A SCHOOL SUBJECT

In a process stretching from the 1890s to the mid-20th century, the social studies curriculum has taken shape. Lasting changes since then, in form and content, have been more additive than they have fundamental alterations. In other words, the basic form of the social studies curriculum emerged by the 1940s.

The Progressive education movement was a pivotal influence on both the social education approach and the social science approach. But social educators tended to be more interested in questions about the individual student and social living than the more subject matter–oriented social science approach. Moreover, adherents to each position have adopted varying stances.

Thus, while social educators embraced the Progressive catch-phrase "social efficiency," different social education proponents meant different things by it. One important strain of social efficiency was articulated by the educational sociologist David Snedden. He construed social education as largely a matter of adapting the student to existing social conditions. "School-promoted learnings," Snedden (1935) wrote, "are to be valued as *means* to the personal and social behaviors which they motivate, initiate and guide" (p. 9). The social studies, in other words, should prepare students for their lives. Therefore social studies programs should be a preplanned study of "two of the great fields of functionings of school acquired learnings which...[may be] dependent upon...the areas of cultural and civic objectives" (p. 13). Unless social studies subject matter served such preformulated ends, Snedden doubted its educational worth (see Curti, 1959, pp. 566–567).

Other proponents of social efficiency adopted far different views of how to educate the individual as well as the character of desirable social arrangements. Notably, John Dewey (1997) argued that the manner in which Snedden was fitting young people to assigned adult roles "result[ed] in subordinating the freedom of the individual to a preconceived social and political status" (p. 18). Although I will not go into Dewey's conception of social education here, I raise his differences with Snedden over the meaning of social efficiency to illustrate that there were competing versions of social education from the outset. Caution is warranted, both in the past and now, when writers proceed as if social education is a singular entity.

Nevertheless, for all their differences, Snedden and Dewey concurred that the curriculum developer should be first of all concerned with the needs of individuals and society and that subject matter from the academic disciplines and elsewhere is selected to serve these purposes. Social scientists tended to approach the matter from the opposite direction. Although social scientists eventually got to the school's societal role, the interests and capacities of pupils, and so forth, these considerations came after the role of subject matter.

For example, the AHA's (1899) Committee of Seven produced perhaps the most widely adopted curriculum recommendations in the history of the social studies. As noted in Chapter 1, their starting point was that education for the demands of contemporary living required the study of history. The Seven observed of the young person, for instance, that "comprehension of the political and social problems that will confront him in everyday life" is "best secured by a study of the past" (pp. 18–19). The great bulk of the Seven's more-than-130-page report is couched in the language of subject matter.

Progressive Era social scientists' view of *professional* knowledge to a great extent was conceived as subject-matter knowledge. Along the same lines, they thought of curriculum improvement in the schools in terms of adapting developments in the academic disciplines. For example, the "new" historians of the Progressive Era added their advocacy of social betterment to the 19th-century common school history curriculum that had been at pains to promote American nationalism (see Moreau, 2003). Other common school-curriculum mainstays such as geography, too, were modernized as the academic discipline changed. The Association of American Geographers, for instance, endorsed the teaching of commercial geography in the schools, at least partly as a result of geographers' developing interest in the growing internationalization of trade (Schulten, 2001, p. 107).

Although social educators may have sometimes ended up with some of the same topics in the curriculum as did social scientists, their rationales stemmed from educational criteria rather than imitation of the disciplines. In this regard, Dewey's views are again illustrative. He forcefully and repeatedly argued that the social sciences had no strong claim on the curriculum unless they were used to illuminate current conditions (Dewey, 1966, 1990, 1991a).

During the Progressive Era, struggles to define the legitimate content of the social studies curriculum often unfolded in the context of national committees such as the aforementioned Committee of Seven created by the AHA. Some of these committees focused on the social studies in elementary education, others in secondary education, while others were restricted to particular disciplinary fields such as history or civics. Although their recommendations differed in some respects, all the committees recognized that the curriculum both needed the content of the social sciences and required a social education rationale (Watras, 2002).

WHERE SHOULD THE CURRICULUM DEVELOPER BEGIN?

Despite broad agreement on the interdependence of social science and social education perspectives in constructing balanced, sound curricula, adherents of each perspective still found plenty to disagree about. Partly these disagreements were about the relative weight assigned to each perspective while other differences were more fundamental. What was and is certain, however, is that curriculum developers must confront these questions anew each time they act. For instance, what we end up teaching in civics depends heavily on whether we first ask what currently is of interest in the discipline of political science or whether we ask what young people need to know to become caring and responsible citizens and what society requires of young people. Moreover, does broad agreement that a knowledge of history and civics is necessary in the education of good citizens imply that they should be combined to address civic problems directly, or are the two subjects best approached as separate entities?

As these questions suggest, different stakeholders in the social studies curriculum might agree on an educational aim such as citizenship but still disagree on how the curriculum should be organized to accomplish it. Consequently, where curriculum developers begin—what questions they first pose about the content and organization of a school program—matters a great deal.

As noted, social scientists have persisted in viewing curriculum making for the schools as essentially simplifying the academic discipline as taught in higher education. To be accurate, however, this disciplinary focus did not necessarily preclude attention to correlated material such as current events (see Wesley, 1944, pp. 61–63). Nevertheless, *social studies* was treated mostly as a convenient collective noun for separate courses in the social sciences and perhaps nondisciplinary courses such as social problems. This emphasis tended to work against both integration of the social sciences and viewing curriculum as a flexible instrument to be significantly adjusted according to the flow of classroom life. Failure to "cover" the preplanned curriculum may be viewed as being "off task" rather than as engagement in a pursuit of emergent educational opportunities.

The discipline-centered model has dominated secondary social studies since the rise of the modern curriculum, as evidenced by high school teachers' often referring to themselves as "history" or "economics" teachers rather than as social studies teachers. Some educators have accused this curricular form of inviting the treatment of young people as novices in the advanced study of the academic disciplines whereby the imperatives of general education may be neglected (e.g., Tyler, 1949, p. 26). Indeed, confusion of specialized and general education seems to account for why some educators (e.g., Bain, 2000) have lamented the "breach" between how history, for example, is approached in schools versus how it is approached in the academy (see Segall, 2002, pp. 10–11).

Since the aim of general education is not to make everyone into scholarly specialists, social educators believe that social scientists often fail to ask the right questions in curriculum development. Surely, at the elementary level, and perhaps also at the secondary level, educational reformers have suggested, the teaching of separate school subjects, with an emphasis on the academic disciplines, may not be what would serve our students and our society best (Sosniak, 1999, p. 191). As Clyde Kohn, former president of both the Association of American Geographers and the National Council for Geographic Education, put it: "What geographers are researching and teaching at a particular time may be of great interest to them and to their professional colleagues, but may not be essential to a sound geographic program at the elementary and secondary grade levels" (cited in Muessig, 1987, p. 528).

Social educators are more concerned with general education than with scholarship in the social sciences per se. The same concern motivates social educators to disregard the boundaries of the social sciences when curriculum integration appears educationally justified. For example, anthropology, current events, geography, and history may be combined in a sixth-grade study of "the peoples and cultures of Mexico."

As mentioned above, just as social scientists may include correlated material such as current events and social problems, social educators draw on the academic disciplines for subject matter. Just because their priority is not in making little disciplinary scholars, this in no way implies that social educators shun the content and methods of the social sciences (Reeder, 1935). Likewise, just because social educators value pursuing emergent opportunities during instruction—what Dewey called flexible purposing—this in no way implies that the curriculum is

unplanned. Indeed, social educators need to plan more thoroughly to be prepared for the various directions classroom encounters
might take.

In practice, the social science and social education approaches
are seldom found in "pure" form. They are archetypes to which
various social studies programs adhere to varying degrees. Still,
they are useful models to ponder as they help us clarify where we
stand educationally. Two significant social studies courses—the
American history survey and Problems of Democracy (POD)—are
representative of the social science and social education approaches, respectively. These two courses are among the most widely
taught and enduring social studies offerings in the history of U.S.
education. They serve to illustrate some typical possibilities and
problems associated with different forms of social studies curriculum.

SOCIAL STUDIES AS SOCIAL SCIENCE:
THE SURVEY OF AMERICAN HISTORY

American history has long been the most widely taught social
studies course. In nearly all states, its teaching is required by law
(see Jenness, 1990, chap. 11). Usually it takes the form of a survey
of American history from its early years to more recent times.
Characteristically it is organized as a narrative of national
progress, with particular attention to landmark developments in
the rise of the nation, such as the Revolution and the
Constitution, the conquest of the West, the Civil War and emancipation, industrialization, reform movements, and the United
States as a world power. The content has changed over time,
reflecting changing scholarship and social conditions, but the
form of the course has been remarkably stable since the early
years of the 20th century (Thornton, 2001c). In addition to courses titled American or U.S. history, a good deal of this material is
included in other courses such as civics and state history. The
integration of American history into other social studies courses—and complaints from critics about American history courses
losing ground in the curriculum—generate controversy from time
to time.

One of the clearest examples of the issues connected with
American history arose during World War II. With the nation's

heritage imperiled by external foes, a media campaign declared a crisis in the teaching of American history. The campaign began when a prominent historian, Allan Nevins (1942) of Columbia University, wrote an article in the *New York Times Magazine.* He charged that, unlike their parents' generation, schoolchildren and college students were not studying American history. He railed against newfangled methods. In effect, Nevins claimed a unifying American history narrative was being supplanted by an integrated "social slush" more concerned with the present than the past.

Social studies educators responded to the campaign with indignation. They found the charges astonishing in their disregard of evidence, as social studies educators were to find at other times with similar attacks by historians on the social studies (e.g., Thornton, 1990). Two of the most prominent social studies educators of the day, Erling Hunt and Edgar B. Wesley, are representative of the response of the social studies community, or at least the engaged leadership part of it. Both men had written extensively and approvingly on the role of history in social studies programs, which apparently added to their astonishment. Hunt, editor of NCSS's official journal, *Social Education,* swiftly used his editor's column to denounce the charges. For instance, he forcefully (and accurately) denied Nevins's central charge that American history had been supplanted by the social studies (Thornton, 1996).

Wesley (1943), a former NCSS president and author of a leading social studies methods textbook, who considered himself a friend of history in the curriculum, took the battle to the historians. Writing in the journal of the Mississippi Valley Historical Association (MVHA, later the Organization of American Historians), Wesley echoed Hunt about history's adequate representation in the curriculum while conceding that it did not always appear in courses labeled *history.* But the problem, Wesley insisted, was not neglect of history but failure to teach it with an eye to its "educative value." Simply transferring the methods of the college historian to schools, Wesley declared, does not motivate students to learn the material. Rather, they required methods that involved utilizing history to some relevant purpose. In other words, Wesley argued that American history courses required a social education rationale if young people were to see its relevance to their lives.

Wesley went on to point out that historians were often quick to criticize school history programs, but were seldom around to make constructive contributions to curriculum-improvement efforts. Moreover, he charged: "Historians have generally slighted their function as the trainer of teachers. The alienation of high school teachers from college teachers frequently begins in the college classroom" (Wesley, 1943, p. 571). Here Wesley was bringing into the open disagreements over social science versus social education, which had usually been muted in public forums.

The public acrimony disturbed both historians and social studies educators. Neither group liked the continuing public trial in the media nor the implications of calls for legislative mandates to require more courses in American history, suggesting loss of professional authority. The three professional groups most directly concerned, AHA, NCSS, and MVHA, moved to reassert their authority.

A committee of historians and social studies educators was convened to investigate and make recommendations. Wesley was appointed to direct the study and the MVHA president and AHA executive secretary served as *ex officio* chairmen (Wesley, 1944). Just as the committee began its work, the controversy again erupted with the publication in *The New York Times* of a narrowly fact-based test administered to 7,000 college freshmen in 36 institutions. The paper's education editor opined that the test results showed a striking ignorance of even the most elementary aspects of United States history (Hertzberg, 1981, p. 69).

The committee conducted a broad-based study, including collecting information from schools, historians, and educators across the nation. Also, a test was administered to various groups, including high-school students, military students, social studies teachers, selected persons listed in *Who's Who in America*, and "selected adults" (see Wesley, 1944, pp. 6–12). Overall, the study was probably the most thorough and balanced investigation of American history in schools and colleges ever conducted.

The main conclusion of the study was that American history was not being neglected and that Americans were not unduly ignorant of their history. The way American history was organized and taught was identified as the principal problem. In contrast to the nationalistic-sounding stance of Nevins and his fellow campaigners, the committee argued against an isolated treatment of American history, preferring to place it in its international setting.

The thrust of the committee's proposals primarily concerned curriculum organization. The members stressed that there was no conflict between the claims of American history and other social studies courses. Both were important (Wesley, 1944, pp. 61–62). There was no hint of the animosity directed toward the social studies courses expressed by Nevins and the *Times*. Since enough American history was being taught, the committee concluded, there was no need for the states to mandate more teaching of it. Indeed, the committee urged that such matters be left to historians and educators, not politicians and bureaucrats.

Specifically on curriculum organization, the committee identified repetition of subject matter across grade levels as a major problem. Conceding that some repetition was inevitable, even desirable, they endorsed continuation of offering American history three times. (These courses were generally offered in Grades 5 or 6 and 7 or 8 and 11 or 12.) But they devised a distinctive approach for each time the course was offered. This was based on child-development considerations (e.g., the material became more abstract as the grade level became higher) and a different chronological focus at each grade level. In ascending grade order, the overarching themes for each course were "How People Live," "The Building of the Nation," and "A Democratic Nation in a World Setting." Each of the three courses would cover the span of American history from Columbus's voyage in 1492; however, two thirds of the elementary and junior high courses would be more focused: on the Colonial and early national periods, and from 1776 to 1876, respectively. In high school, half the course was devoted to the period since 1865 (Wesley, 1944, pp. 70–71).

While local adaptations were mentioned as possibilities, Wesley's report obviously supported a largely ready-made and standardized program of study. The theme for each grade was broken down into recommended topics, representative dates and persons, and skills to be emphasized. For the upper elementary grades, for example, the first item in each of the aforementioned categories, respectively, was: "Exploration of the hemisphere," "Discovery of America, 1492," "Daniel Boone," and "The use of table of contents, paragraph and section headings, and index for efficient location of material in books."

Although the report explicitly eschewed treatment of classroom methods (claiming inadequate resources), it nonetheless held a number of important implications for them. For example, the committee members recommended enrichment of the suggested content with material drawn from the regional, state, and local scene. They also suggested that current events should be taught for both their own sake and as a standard of measurement of the pertinence of the history that had been taught. Other points suggestive for method included emphasis on critical thinking, depth of study rather than superficial coverage, the aforementioned international rather than narrowly national perspective, and a recognition that study of the ideals and traditions of democracy requires attention to social and economic as well as political history. In this list, there was clearly a hefty overlap of social science and social education.

While the committee adopted a broader view of the proper scope of American history in particular and the social studies curriculum in general than social science alone, they emphatically endorsed the social studies as a federation of subjects rather than as the integration of them. They observed that "very seldom does a teacher try to teach the whole *field* [social studies] as a single course, but he tries constantly to show the interrelations of the subjects within the field" (Wesley, 1944, pp. 56–57).

Perhaps the influence of the historians on the committee, the largely prepackaged conception of curriculum that seemed to be taken for granted, the charge to focus on history, or some combination thereof explains why their focus for teacher education involved courses in the social sciences. Too much time in teacher education programs, the committee alleged, was spent on education courses at the expense of the social sciences. Although education courses were deemed necessary, the committee sounded more enthusiastic when it turned to remedying the shortcomings of teachers in the social sciences. The committee expressed no special interest in how social studies teacher education as whole should be conceived. They did note, however, that the subject matter demands of teaching limited the usefulness of highly specialized social science courses. Recognizing that social studies teachers were responsible for broad swathes of subject matter in general education, rather than the specialized courses that social science professors might prefer to teach, they recommended courses such as "New Viewpoints in History" and "The Idea of a World State" as suitable in "both depth and breadth" (Wesley, 1944, p. 107).

The committee's recommendations for American history contrast with those of the influential 1916 NEA Committee on Social Studies (NEA, 1994). For example, the 1916 report deliberately "refrained from offering detailed outlines of courses, on the ground that they tend to fix instruction in stereotyped forms inconsistent with a real socializing purpose" (p. 10). Instead, they had provided a mere three lessons to illustrate what they had in mind for high school history courses, versus the lists of specified information and skills provided by the 1944 group. A further difference is that the American history report (Wesley, 1944) treats the social studies subjects less as an integrated field than as distinct entities.

Perhaps the American history report could be considered a model by which the social sciences and the social education positions could coexist in a comprehensive view of the social studies. Its curricular rationale for American history is an interesting attempt at balancing subject-specific and broader goals. American history, the report says, makes well-rounded citizens and good neighbors—standard social studies goals whatever the course. But history also teaches an important way of thinking, the report continues, that cannot be secured any other way than through the study of history as a distinct subject. This, too, is offset as the report notes: "Faith in the efficacy of history...does not mean any disparagement of civics or economics or geography or sociology" (Wesley, 1944, pp. 61–62).

Whatever its strengths, however, the American history report does not appear to have had great effects on practice (Gross, 1958, p. 214). The report's sponsors—the two historians' groups and NCSS—endorsed the report. All three groups agreed to implement the report, although, not surprisingly, the school-oriented NCSS took the lead (Hertzberg, 1981, p. 71). In particular, NCSS devoted its yearbook (Thursfield, 1947) to the American history report with a highly useful and comprehensive treatment of its meaning for aims, content, methods and materials, and assessment in American history and the other social studies. The report aroused more modest interest among historians. As often happens with compromises, surface-level agreement concealed lingering disagreements. Hunt (1944), for example, found the report's suggestions for curriculum reorganization constructive and seemed to appreciate that his main criticism of the history campaigners had been vindicated by the nationwide investigation of American history programs showing enough of the subject was taught. Nevertheless, he quibbled with some points and expressed disappointment at the report's failure to declare that the entire set of criticisms by the history campaigners had been invalid in the first place. On the other hand, some "conservative" historians were displeased, with one grumbling, for instance, that too much had been conceded to "the educationalists" (Novick, 1988, p. 370).

Looking back from the 21st century, the American history report is perhaps most interesting as an episode in the growing gulf between academic historians and educators who were concerned with the teaching of the social sciences in the schools. As the reader will recall, this was not new in the 1940s: Wesley (1943) had complained of historians' well-established indifference to helping the schools before the national investigation and committee work began. The AHA's representative on the board of NCSS's journal, *Social Education*, noted a similar distancing, remarking that his organization's interest "in the direction of and leadership of instruction" was "virtually surrendered" between the 1930s and late 1940s. Similarly, in 1947 the other major historians' group, the Mississippi Valley Historical Association, discontinued the teacher's section in its journal (cited in Novick, 1988, p. 368).

Although social studies educators and social scientists, especially historians, had frequently worked in close partnership during the Progressive Era, by the mid-20th century, higher education rewarded social scientists for depth rather than breadth in scholarship. Whatever they once may have done, social scientists largely disclaimed responsibility for attending to the subject matter demands of school teaching in their courses (Shaver, 1985). At the same time, the old teachers' colleges, with their union of content and method, were rapidly disappearing. School people were still expected to organize broad, synthetic courses, but social science professors increasingly jockeyed to offer undergraduate colloquia in their research specialties rather than broad-based courses (Cuban, 1999). Teacher education may have gained in status by moving from teachers' colleges to liberal arts colleges and universities; but it lost also, because there were fewer mechanisms or incentives for anyone to take a comprehensive view of teacher education (Thornton, 2001a). Social scientists' ignorance of the realities of schooling has, as during the New Social Studies movement of the 1960s, presented a formidable obstacle to their effective participation in curriculum reform.

There is also considerable irony attached to the gulf between social scientists and social studies educators, as more than casual involvement in curriculum work for the schools often results in social scientists' adopting views they had rejected when looking out from the academy. Historians have been the most obvious, but not the only, example of this phenomenon, as pointed out by the "court historian" of the last national commission on social studies, which recommended a history-centered social studies curriculum (see Jenness, 1990, pp. 296–297). As curriculum historian Joseph Watras (2002) puts it, historians who argue against "social studies" end up advocating the same thing once they engage in serious curriculum deliberation:

> Although many historians claim that historians and social studies educators began to go in different directions during World War I and finally split apart during the Great Depression, that was not what happened. Social studies educators and historians had more similar aims and methods than such an argument allows. What is fascinating is that the debate between historians and social studies educators continues, despite the similarity of their views. (pp. 249–250)

This story of apparently great differences but more similarity than is conceded arises again in the following section with the Problems of Democracy course. Although created as the archetypal social studies course conspicuously centered on social problems rather than a particular academic discipline, in practice its aims and methods may not be as different from courses such as the American history survey as has been supposed. Again, teachers as gatekeepers seem to account for a great deal of this similarity.

SOCIAL STUDIES AS SOCIAL EDUCATION: PROBLEMS OF DEMOCRACY

Problems of Democracy (POD)—and its variants such as Problems of American Democracy, American Problems, and American Life and Problems—are quintessential social education courses. Invented by the NEA's 1916 Committee on Social Studies (NEA, 1994), POD was designed as the capstone course for the senior year of high school. It was assigned "the purpose of giving more definite, comprehensive and deeper knowledge of some of the vital problems of social life, and thus securing a more intelligent and active citizenship"(p. 49). The committee believed that no single social science was suited to this important task: "The purposes of secondary education and not the intrinsic value of any particular body of knowledge should be the determining consideration" (p. 53). In other words, the aims of the course were judged incompatible with a prepackaged, social science form of organization.

As envisaged, teacher planning of a POD course was necessarily ad hoc, since which problems would be of interest at any given time could not be entirely foreseen. This also meant that each time a teacher taught the course, much of the preparation could be new. The problems studied were supposed to be approached through the perspectives of economics, sociology, and political science. The committee presented "the problem of immigration" as an example. They specified several economic, sociological, and political "relations of immigration" such as to the problem of land tenure in the United States, to social contributions of immigrants, and to problems of municipal government arising from or complicated by immigration, respectively (p. 51).

The committee recognized that the problems studied would naturally vary over time and from one class of pupils to another. The problems were supposed to be selected (just as the committee had recommended for the selection of subject matter for history and civics) based on their immediate interest to the class as well as their vital importance to society. The committee was basically mute on just how such a course should be organized or in what specific ways it related to preceding courses such as American history. Nor did the committee have much to say on how teachers who had been educated in more established ways would best adapt or be educated for an innovation such as POD.

Social education enthusiasts such as Harold Rugg, joined by political scientists and sociologists who were possibly pleased to have a larger stake in the school curriculum, quickly and enthusiastically promoted POD. As a harbinger of things to come, however, the AHA balked at accepting the course. Nevertheless, POD won rapid acceptance in the schools. By

1924, POD was taught in more schools than medieval history, world history, English history, or sociology. Among social studies courses, by 1928, POD ranked in enrollment second only to American history (Singleton, 1980, pp. 93–94).

Meanwhile, members of AHA and some other social scientists, especially geographers (Schulten, 2001, pp. 123–125), were coming to see social education or even "social studies" as distinct from courses in the individual social sciences as a curricular rival. Would their subjects be swallowed up by an integrated curriculum? Would an interactive approach downgrade disciplinary content in social studies courses? The prospect of an affirmative answer to either question was probably remote; many leaders of NCSS also favored a curriculum centered on a prepackaged, social science approach. Moreover, courses such as state and U.S. history were often mandated by the states, required for college admission, or both. Nevertheless, AHA was sufficiently concerned to convene a panel of prominent social scientists and educators to make recommendations on the social studies in the schools.

At the close of the 1920s, AHA moved to establish the Commission on the Social Studies, expecting, as a matter of course, that it would favor history (and possibly other social sciences). This plan backfired (Lagemann, 1992). While the commission failed to formulate a recommended scope and sequence of courses, most of its members, both social scientists and educators, endorsed social studies. Exactly what they meant by endorsing the social studies was arguably less than clear in the absence of the commission's recommending a scope and sequence; nonetheless, the endorsement displeased both traditional historians as well as educators who favored social sciences rather than social education. The traditionalists among the historians and educators objected that the social studies methods endorsed would undermine the integrity of the individual subjects. In addition, a sizable number of educators were concerned with more or less the opposite issue—that the commission's recommendations were too general and theoretical to effect concrete changes in methods along the lines that the commission seemed to be advocating (e.g., Haggerty, 1935).

Aside from traditional historians' hostility to the type of course of which POD was an archetype, POD's widespread adoption did not mean its implementation went smoothly. Although there are documented cases of its functioning successfully (Hoffenbacher, 1958), POD presented formidable organizational difficulties. The course's formulators (NEA, 1994) may be presumed to be the legitimate authority on its proper form, but they offered only the barest outline of what POD should look like.

The questions and dilemmas presented because POD had been so sketchily described were often left to practitioners to resolve as the POD course was implemented. For example, teachers were left to answer what should be done if the immediate interests of students failed to coincide with significant societal problems. How, and by whom, were they to be reconciled? Was the course meant to be sequential, with a steady accumulation of skills and information, or a series of discrete units differing largely by topic? Where were teachers supposed to find the time, energy, imagination, and materials required for a course that substantially differed each time it was offered?

Although the empirical evidence about what happened in classrooms is limited (e.g., Cornett, 1990), POD eventually seems to have fallen into standard patterns of social studies courses, not necessarily emphasizing problem solving. Instruction centered on the means of conveying information, such as textbooks and worksheets, simplifies teachers' planning responsibilities, can be used semester after semester, clarifies the tasks students will be expected to perform, and makes evaluation of what has been learned relatively straightforward and "objective" (Eisner, 1985, p. 110). These features sit comfortably with the culture of American schooling (McNeil, 1986). But the idea of textbook-driven instruction in POD appears incongruent and may be in some respects a violation of the course's intended orientation, whereby subject matter would emerge partly through inquiry into problems not previously identified.

Nevertheless, demands for POD textbooks were heeded and teachers received them despite the evident danger that the transmission of fixed bodies of information rather than problem solving would become the focus of the course. Dewey (1991a) chided that such methods and materials of instruction in social studies courses such as POD undermined the aims they were supposedly directed toward. In such reduced form, he warned, the social studies were only crowding an already overburdened school curriculum.

In retrospect, it seems wholly understandable that the organizational demands of POD as originally conceived overwhelmed many teachers, and they responded by retreating to possibly less-than-ideal, but nonetheless tried-and-true, instructional methods and materials. Rugg (1936) saw this problem more clearly than did many educators. Although a great enthusiast of the problems approach to social studies instruction, Rugg was nonetheless a realist about the circumstances of classroom teachers. He concluded that it is unrealistic to expect teachers to engage in spontaneous curriculum-making and expect a well-organized, sequential, and substantive product. "The inevitable result" of spontaneous curriculum-making, Rugg wrote, "with a broad curriculum and thirty to fifty young people has been educational chaos" (p. 345).

POD was conceived as an experiment in social education. It is nonetheless evident that the course often turned out more like social science courses than its theoretical basis would have predicted. It appears that forces such as gatekeeping propel social studies courses—whatever they are called or whether they favor social science or social education—in some significantly similar directions.

This is both good and bad news. It is clearly the latter for social science or social education purists; however, as I have already noted, purists in the social sciences normally ended up embracing social education goals as well. The same may be true the other way round, that is, that thoughtful enthusiasts for problem-centered instruction ended up realizing that it places enormous demands on mastery of social science methods and knowledge. Rugg (1939) spoke to how his problem-based curriculum increased the need for knowledge from the traditional academic subjects such as history (p. 156) (although, as I take up in Chapter 6, this knowledge may not be isomorphic with the current interests of historians).

The good news may be that often the rhetoric of social science versus social education is shriller than the real differences between positions, as fair-minded observers mentioned already such as Watras (2002) and Jenness (1990) have forcefully argued. As the chapters in the second part of this book reveal, the interdependence of the social science and social education perspectives is so great that it is hard to imagine a defensible curriculum without a strong element of both. It is a matter of bringing them together in ways that are consonant with the aims we profess, which is the subject of the following chapter, and with organizing curricular-instructional arrangements and teacher education accordingly, the subject of the second half of the book.

3   *Aims Must Matter*

In Chapter 1, the history of aims talk in social studies was introduced. In this chapter I build on that foundation, arguing that aims talk is indispensable for educators at all levels, including classroom teachers. Unlike the Progressive Era, or decades thereafter for that matter, aims talk has not been a conspicuous feature of American education since the rise of the standards movement in the 1990s. Instead, it is assumed that the aims of education are settled and geared toward individual and national economic betterment and that traditional academic subjects such as history and geography are the only effective means to reach these aims. I think that both these assumptions are radically incomplete, and I will argue (as did Dewey) that there is no surer road to educational problems than teachers who do not understand the purposes of their actions. Moreover, I insist that any adequate conception of social studies aims must attend to more than the current interests of scholars in the traditional academic subjects, upon which the standards pertaining to the social studies curriculum were largely based.

AIMS TALK MATTERS

By *aims*, I mean the broad purposes that school programs are supposed to accomplish. For example, school mission statements and state curriculum frameworks regularly proclaim "citizenship" to be a fundamental aim. In theory, the goals of particular courses, such as U.S. history, are based on these broader aims. In turn, the specific objectives of units of instruction and lessons, which normally teachers devise, are supposed to be derived from course goals. The linkages between these three levels of educational purpose, however, are usually poorly articulated or not specified at all in practice. Even more seldom are they monitored or evaluated in schools.

Many teachers do not feel personal or professional responsibility for aims talk and may even be impatient with hearing about it (Noddings, 2003a, p. 76). After all, persons with authority usually formulate aims in distant places. Who is the classroom teacher to question this? By the same token, teacher-preparation programs may provide scant attention to aims talk—in contrast to more microlevel formulation of instructional objectives—tacitly conveying that grandiose decisions provide a framework within which teachers work but over which they have no real power. But if the notion of gatekeeping is taken seriously, neither of these two responses will suffice.

Some years ago, Charles Silberman (1970) studied and wrote during another period when American education was widely judged to be in deep trouble. Contrary to his long-held beliefs, Silberman eventually concluded that the central educational problems confronted in the 1960s and 1970s were to do with a disconnection between the aims announced for education and the goals and objectives actually pursued. More generously than many of today's educational critics, he did not attribute this state of affairs to educators' "venality or indifference or stupidity, but to mindlessness" (p. 10).

As noted in the Introduction, Silberman's line of thought was picked up a few years later by President James Shaver (1977) of the NCSS, who echoed Silberman's remark on mindlessness. Shaver charged that social studies gatekeeping was mired in unexamined practices. These practices, whether "workable" or not, had lost touch with why social studies was taught in the first place. For example, U.S. history courses are supposed to cultivate critical thinking, thus educating a more aware and informed citizenry. But as experienced at the classroom level, these courses may place a premium on short-term memorization of information. There is no reason to think that this state of affairs has markedly improved since Shaver spoke; indeed, it seems more likely that it has worsened with the subsequent ascendance of standards and tests. Even the prominence of accountability mechanisms such as standards and tests, powerful as they undoubtedly can be (see Kohn, 2004), does not obviate the need for aims talk. Much of the time significant degrees of teacher discretion remain. As S.G. Grant (2003) points out, mechanisms such as tests do not dictate teacher behavior. Rather, they interact with other elements of teacher gatekeeping (p. 114). And, it is worth remembering that the history of educational change suggests the accountability movement, like so many other movements, may itself diminish over time.

Given the sometimes profound dissonance between the aims we profess and the practices we embrace, aims talk is not a luxury in which only outside "experts" and ivory-tower academics—who have time on their hands—engage, but is essential for thoughtful classroom teaching. It is vital in teaching, curriculum work, and teacher education.

Unless educators at all levels engage in aims talk, the purposes of education become submerged and the aims originally conceived may be lost. Digital technology in recent years provides an apt point of comparison where ends have frequently been forgotten in the pursuit of means. Internet access for schools, for instance, was touted as a national imperative before most teachers had much idea what educational uses to put it to. "We have tended," environmental educator David W. Orr (2002) writes, "to become technological fundamentalists, unwilling, perhaps unable, to question our basic assumptions about how our tools relate to our larger purposes and prospects" (p. 63).

Three main sources of aims are commonly used: the interests and aptitudes of students, the demands of social living, and contemporary scholarship. Although these sources overlap, neglect of one or two of them, as in the structure of the disciplines movement of the 1960s, may lead to unbalanced school programs (see Goodlad, 1966). For example, observers criticized most of the New Social Studies programs of the time, which were single-mindedly academic, because they made little provision for the here-and-now problems facing youngsters in their own personal circumstances (Longstreet, 1973, p. 264).

Although each source of aims needs attention, aims are broad statements of educational aspiration and, hence, may suggest various possibilities for goals and objectives. Social aims, for example, may result in priorities for fitting the child into the existing social order, for educating young people to act as social reformers, or somewhere in between. What seems clear, however, is that all curricula explicitly or implicitly convey some message about society, even if it is the view often tacit in New Social Studies materials that educators should concentrate on the dispassionate study of society. Aims, albeit perhaps tacitly, are at work whether we like it or not.

THE STUDENT AS A SOURCE OF AIMS

School programs are based on the assumption that their content and methods are somehow "good" for young people. One manifestation of this assumption is the oft-stated aspiration to develop each child's potential to the fullest. Such a purpose is plainly open to numerous reasonable interpretations. Should the child's potential be nudged toward parental hopes, toward the child's innate aptitudes, toward competence in subject matters that scholars deem significant, or in other directions? In any case, considering the student as a source of aims concerns at least three matters about each student: needs, interests, and aptitudes. I'll begin with needs, because the belief that schooling is "good" for young people presupposes that it meets their needs in some way.

Immediately, we are confronted with defining what we mean by *needs*, a term that is as ubiquitous in educational discourse as its meaning is imprecise. In its most basic sense, *needs* refers to what is indispensable to an individual. Biological needs are the most pressing, since everyone requires food, water, shelter, and safety in order to lead even a minimally acceptable life. Although these needs are fundamental—except in cases where, say, children come to school ill nourished or are the subject of bullying—biological needs are not usually the main ones social studies educators are concerned with. Thus, while acknowledging that these needs must be met before educational experiences are likely to be effectual, I'll move on to educational needs.

If our aim is to develop each child's potential to the fullest, we must confront questions such as, What are the educational needs of each student? How similar are they from one person to another? Who decides what they are? Honestly answering these questions reveals that no two children will have identical needs. This is important to keep in mind because discussions of needs have often been couched in terms of groups of students (e.g., Tyler, 1949). Even in tracked classes where students exhibit great similarities, the needs of one individual in a class may vary significantly from the needs of another student.

There are two main kinds of needs that are relevant to my purposes here: those expressed by the child and those inferred by others (Noddings, 2002b). Expressed needs in social studies may take the form of a student's request for help with map skills as this area of weakness is holding up his or her progress in geography. More often in schooling, however, educators infer the needs of their pupils. For example, a teacher may see the need for a student to have more practice in structuring essays before an impending test; or when students are studying difficult primary sources, a student who lacks English proficiency may be paired with another student whose first language is English. Sometimes teachers may infer at the spur of the moment that student needs have changed. For example, a teacher may capitalize on some unforeseen remark as an opportunity to revitalize student interest in a lesson. Although it may seem a random occurrence (how could you anticipate the unforeseen?), teachers who spontaneously change course may be acting from fine-tuned inferences about student needs. Rather than this being serendipity, David Hawkins (1973) calls it planning for spontaneity.

In addition to particular skills and student curiosity, teachers infer needs in terms of what an individual student may or may not profit from. For example, even if a student finds constructing maps tedious and uninteresting, the teacher may have to explain that it is essential for further work in geography. Alternatively, a teacher may tell a student who has no intrinsic interest in the legacy of ancient Rome and does not plan to pursue further work in history what minimally must be learned for passing the course. As a variation on these two references to student interest, it could be argued that students have a need for promoting their interest with vital subject matter. In other words, teachers will ordinarily do their best to encourage intrinsic interest in vital subject matter, as interest is central to growing competence in any subject.

A still more important need than competence with given bodies of subject matter may be developing students' powers of inquiry. Jerome Bruner's (1960) dictum that students should learn how to learn remains valid. Learning about learning, however, may as much depend on the implicit curriculum of classroom routines as be a matter of the formal curriculum or direct instruction. For example, penalizing guessing in classroom discussions discourages students from learning to develop and test hypotheses. Instead, teachers might encourage taking intellectual risks. Teachers can also encourage such inquiry-directed thinking by their own hypothesizing about questions asked by the class and by subjecting these guesses to visible critical analysis.

The development of powers of inquiry seems to be threatened, however, by levels of specificity in learning standards conceived in the 1990s. Moving directly to inculcating predetermined lists of facts and relationships is an educational mistake if the step of arousing student curiosity is skipped. Whitehead (1929) called this step the stage of romance: "Education must essentially be a setting in order of a ferment already stirring in the mind: you cannot educate mind in *vacuo*" (p. 29). The vital "rhythm" of education, he warned, is disrupted by moving to the stage of precision, that is, specific facts and relationships, without a previous state of romance.

Two objections are commonly raised when student interest is suggested as a valid source of aims. Both are real obstacles to the method I'm proposing, but they are seldom insurmountable (Thornton, 2001b). First, critics contend that with a class of 30 or so students (and possibly five different courses per day), how can a teacher address individual interests? One method may be to provide limited choices. Imagine a teacher who has taught the same European history course for several years. While there will likely be material about Nazi Germany that the teacher will expect every student to cover—perhaps the construction of a police state, anti-Semitic policies, and an expansionist foreign policy—each student might be permitted to study in depth one topic that holds special interest for him or her. If this proves too taxing for the teacher's available time and energy or materials are limited, perhaps four or five choices about Nazi Germany could be managed (e.g., women's lives, autobahns and cars, air raids during the war, Nazi administration of occupied countries, or relations with the Vatican). Although no one of these topics may be a perfect fit with the interests of every student, the chances are that some will hold interest, or interest will develop, for a significant number of students.

The second objection is that content standards and associated high-stakes tests constrain choice. To varying extents, this is true. But again it does not have to be a matter of no choice versus the choice of whatever interests students. (Indeed, I would argue that both ends of this dichotomy may be equally undesirable. For instance, young people almost invariably require some direction from teachers to ensure that their studies are progressing toward desirable ends, just as good teachers try to seize opportunities to individualize subject matter.) Even when the content and skills to be covered are specified in some detail, as in the case of the New York State global history and geography curriculum, thoughtful teachers find ways for more in-depth study to stimulate student interests (MacDonald, 2003). There usually is no good reason why some material a student encounters cannot be a matter of individual choice.

For example, a required topic such as India in a global history and geography course often devolves into a survey of abstracted generalizations about geography and politics divorced from the concrete realities of everyday life. But it can be studied from vantage points of everyday life such as workplaces, family life, architecture, foods, gender relations, and so on. This provides opportunities for choice from readily accessible concepts. Eventually, with proper direction, any of these vantage points will lead to an overall picture. For example, a thoughtful treatment of gender relations will quickly lead to considerations of religion, dress, diet, occupations, politics, and so on. As in the teaching of the antebellum period of U.S. history, beginning with treatment of an enslaved female or Lowell mill girl leads incvitably to the treatment of Abraham Lincoln, but if the unit begins with Lincoln, the student may never get to the enslaved female or mill girl (see Crocco, 1997).

Young people are mostly interested in subject matter for which they have aptitude and vice versa. Nonetheless, the teacher is responsible for raising possibilities that their students may otherwise overlook. That is, students may have aptitude for, say, economics, but unless the student is exposed to economic subject matter the student may be unaware of his or her aptitude. Sometimes, however, students may have great interest in a topic but their aptitude for its study or the prerequisites for its study may be inadequate. For example, a student may have a great curiosity about archeological artifacts from ancient times but be lacking in other qualities that might lead to a successful career in that field. In such cases, a teacher could counsel other lines of work where the student would still be able to interact with ancient artifacts, perhaps employment in a museum setting or at an Internet site.

The needs, interests, and aptitudes of students ought to be part of aims talk if we are serious about "leaving no child behind." Current learning standards do a great disservice if standardization of the curriculum edges out opportunities for individualization of the curriculum. Young people learn most effectively and enthusiastically material that is connected to their personal experience and aspirations. Without consideration of individual differences, standards conceived to increase U.S. economic competitiveness and pass along an agreed-upon body of knowledge may have the opposite effect than that of raising academic standards for all. Simply declaring that "this material is good for all students" does not make it so. Where we can, we should capitalize on individual strengths rather than wastefully ignoring them.

SOCIETY AS A SOURCE OF AIMS

More than any other school subject, by definition the *social* studies look to society as a source of aims. "From the nature of their content," as the 1916 NEA Committee on Social Studies put it, "the social studies afford peculiar opportunities for training of the individual as a member of society" (NEA, 1994). Similarly, it was noted in the AHA's Commission on Social Studies volume on curriculum development:

> Their [social studies] essential task in our schools—attended by many, worthy collateral purposes—is to aid youth to the fullest practicable understanding of our social order; to the meaningful realization of the ways in which the individual, both pupil and adult, may participate effectively in that order; and to motivation for effective participation. (Marshall & Goetz, 1936, p. 2)

But what type of aims the demands of society imply is not self-evident. Perhaps more than aims concerning the individual or scholarship, social aims have tended to attract controversy outside educational circles. Curriculum-makers may, therefore, exercise some care in formulating social aims. Nevertheless, many such aims appear innocuous enough.

Take, for example, the aim of preparing young people for the social demands of living. Does this imply fitting students into the existing social order or preparing them to change their society? Economic subject matter well illustrates how the aims driving subject matter selection can lead to its serving contrasting purposes. One social justification for economics is its important role in educating intelligent consumers. In Philadelphia, for instance, young people are schooled in "financial literacy" in order to be able to make a personal budget, appreciate the value of saving, and recognize unscrupulous financial practices (Snyder, 2003).

It seems reasonable that schools should provide financial education for young people who might otherwise not encounter it. Perhaps the most likely objection would come from traditional liberal arts–oriented critics who might maintain that financial education should occur in the home or it will be learned anyway in the course of daily living—precious school time should be reserved for academics unlikely to be learned anywhere else. Financial matters may be learned outside school; however, this may be contingent on factors such as social class. Such learning seems more likely to be available in affluent suburban communities than in inner cities. In these poorer communities, financial education may well be more a valuable social education than much of the remote material demanded by standards in, say, world history. Individuals may improve their lives through financial education.

Arguing for the social relevance of financial education or even the relative worth of remote topics in world history, however, is in no way an argument against all young people studying how the U.S. and global order operate. Young people need to encounter how power, wealth, and status are unequally distributed and why, for instance. Particularly, they need to learn to think critically about such material. It is not as if there is a choice of whether to introduce young people to how the world does and ought to work. They will learn to construct their explanations from somewhere. Even students who perceive themselves as marginal to societal power structures sense to some degree that official versions of knowledge presented in social studies lessons may serve the interests of the privileged more than the interests of disadvantaged groups (Epstein, 2001; Valenzuela, 1999, p. 212).

In a balanced social studies program, both adaptation to and criticism of existing social arrangements should find a place. Consider, for instance, the timely topic of globalization. Both the volume of world trade and the mobility of millions of people have been increased by globalization. The consequent greater wealth and opportunities thus created are apparently considerable. Nevertheless, the benefits of globalization have accrued disproportionately to the world's "haves"; the "have-nots" have, instead, often been assured of eventual benefits. In the meantime, manufacturing workers in the U.S. have lost their jobs to lower-wage competition, environmental standards have been compromised, and the doctrine of "open markets" has not extended to the agricultural sectors of the world's wealthiest trading blocs: the

United States, the European Union, and Japan. By the same token, migration for employment and other disruptions of traditional communities have severed connections to place, which may be vital to human flourishing (Gruenwald, 2003; Noddings, 2003a).

Attention to social aims, especially if it results in, say, critical treatment of current problems such as globalization, may arouse controversy. Even when local conditions curtail teacher freedom to deal with current problems, social aims can still be grappled with in standard courses such as U.S. history and government. Consider, for example, subject matter about important business leaders during the Industrial Revolution. This could be studied as the story of "the robber barons," the great industrialists such as Rockefeller and Carnegie who exploited the American public and workers. These same men, however, could be approached as "captains of industry," the makers of modern American economic greatness. In a fair-minded approach, some attention would be given to each story and some attention paid to appraisal of the veracity of each position. Both short- and long-run factors should be considered. Surely in such a treatment, some opportunities would arise for comparisons with present-day conditions concerning the winners and losers of globalization.

Social aims speak most of all to educating an informed and caring citizenry. A hallmark of such citizenship is learning to cope with society as it is and envisaging how society might be improved. Both require the ability to think for one's self. In this sense, social aims are very much intertwined with individual aims. As Dewey (1990) expressed it, "Only by being true to the full growth of all individuals who make it up, can society by any chance be true to itself" (p. 7).

SCHOLARSHIP AS A SOURCE OF AIMS

It is interesting to consider that many people equate scholarship and the content of school programs. While they obviously overlap, scholarly content must first pass through educational tests before it, out of the universe of possible scholarly content, qualifies as subject matter (Thornton, 2001b). Nothing in the content of scholarly knowledge in, say, geography or history intrinsically marks it as material schoolchildren ought to study. These are educational decisions, not scholarly ones. As Jane White

(1987) has pointed out, the teacher is a "broker of scholarly knowledge."

Thus our reasons for teaching what we teach in courses such as U.S. history owe a great deal to addressing the demands of social living and the aptitudes and interests of the individual student. We study the civil rights movement of the mid-20th century partly because historians consider it an important topic in U.S. history, but we also study it because the demands of society suggest its pertinence to race relations, affirmative action, political dissent, and a host of other social and individual aims in the present.

Philosopher of education Jonas Soltis (1968) used the Civil War to explain ways in which a body of scholarly knowledge serves as a "vehicle" for other purposes:

> [We engage in] teaching the facts about the Civil War (x) so that our students can understand the current problems of segregation in the United States (y)....There are many facts about the Civil War, but some are more relevant to our y (problems of segregation) than others. Similarly, once we select those that are most relevant (it would be impossible to teach all the facts about the Civil War), then we have a guideline for organizing these facts in a way which will best achieve our y.
>
> Finally we can test not only for x, but also for what we were ultimately after, the y. (pp. 33–34)

Even Mortimer Adler (1982), who insisted on one academic program of studies for all young people, based his argument on the utility of such a curriculum for a democratic society. Perhaps the closest that K–12 schooling comes to providing scholarly knowledge for its own sake is in courses intended to substitute for college courses, such as advanced placement courses. Specialized courses should, of course, find a place in school programs. But such courses are properly regarded as electives rather than as fundamental to general education. As Ralph Tyler (1949) argued, the contribution of subject-specialist scholars to general education ought to concern what "the subject can contribute to the education of young people who are not going to be specialists in [that] field; What can your subject contribute to the layman, the garden variety of citizen?" (p. 26).

Scholarship should inform social studies programs, however, in another important sense beyond that of general education: studies for the deeply interested. Although most students will be in social studies courses for purposes of general education, some young people are (or may become) fascinated by the subject matter or just desire advanced work. Courses—and perhaps project-type work as well—should be made available to these young people who can pursue ideas and intellectual processes in depth. For able students, this kind of opportunity for sustained work in realms they love may be the most productive part of their entire school experience. Moreover, such specialized work need not, as some may fear, be excessively narrow; as Whitehead (1929) pointed out, "The external connections of the subject drag thought outwards" (p. 18).

Before leaving this chapter on aims and moving to the process of curriculum making, it should be reiterated that the high price of avoiding aims talk may be the loss of our deepest-seated educational aspirations in the daily grind of classrooms. This can, and does, result in jarring incongruities between what we say we want to accomplish and the purposes we actually pursue. Speaking in this regard, Dewey (1966) warned about how history and geography lost their educational purpose if, as frequently happens, social studies are reduced to compilations of information. Instead, he insisted that the function of these subjects "is to enrich and liberate the more direct and personal contacts of life by furnishing their context, their background and outlook" (p. 211). Elaborating on Dewey, Noddings (1995) wrote that history and geography "should enter the curriculum as a way of explaining human activity, enlarging social connections, or solving social problems" (p. 37).

Unless we keep these perspectives in mind—even to the extent possible in the constrained circumstances under which so many educators must work in overregulated schools—schooling and education can become two very different entities. The curriculum, the subject of the following chapter, needs to be designed with this caution in mind.

4

Toward a Balanced and Flexible Curriculum

As may be apparent from my argument so far, conceiving a model for curriculum planning that is flexible enough for a variety of settings and comprehensive enough to accommodate a range of views of social studies curriculum can be a challenge. Embracing too many purposes can result in an incoherent curriculum or simply swamp effective instruction, dangers evident with both the behavioral-objectives movement of the 1960s and 1970s and the content standards devised in the 1990s. Moreover, many of the debates about social studies aims, as discussed in Chapter 3, are pitched at the level of what schools ideally should do, which is vital but nevertheless too general to guide curriculum decision-making at the local level. Awareness that we should aim to teach critical thinking, for instance, is relatively unhelpful for planning courses or lessons unless it is broken down into more manageable components. Although the boundaries are porous to some degree, I will distinguish aims from goals. I use goals to mean the purposes of courses or sequences of courses. Objectives I associate with lessons or sequences of lessons.

Providing a curriculum that young people find relevant to their lives is, as noted, one widely held aim for the social studies curriculum (and for schooling in general). Whereas aims speak to what schools ideally should do, goals are more specifically about what we expect or ask schools to do (see Goodlad, 1994, p. 2). In the 1970s, for instance, relevance was a popular aim, and what goals it implied for a values clarification course may have been evident enough; however, what did it connote for a long-established course such as American history? One answer was in a NCSS yearbook (Kownslar, 1974b) that suggested teaching American history ought to be a "quest for relevancy." Thus, if course goals were taken to include making connections between historical subject matter and issues students face in their daily lives, what topics are best suited to this purpose? What kinds of learning opportunities might lead students to see the relevance of, say, the topic of immigration? What does our goal suggest about how much latitude students should be given in selecting topics of special interest for in-depth study?

In this chapter I ask what, in practice, our chief goals are in social studies and how they inform developing a curriculum. I try to provide an inclusive answer, one that is flexible enough for educators with a range of purposes. I then turn to how different types of goals are related and how balance among them can be secured. Again, I leave open the possibility that these questions can be answered in a range of defensible ways. Finally, I look more explicitly at what role the teacher can play in curriculum planning.

CONCEPTUALIZING CURRICULUM PLANNING

Leading curriculum scholars have long recognized that teachers are seldom adequately trained for either implementing ready-made materials or making their own high-quality materials (Noddings, 1979). It is therefore not surprising that teachers seem to lack conviction about what to teach and how to teach it (p. 302). But just such conviction is required if improvements are to be effected in common but less-than-ideal curricular-instructional arrangements. Exhortation and coercion cannot produce this conviction (Noddings, 2001). Rather, it will require a shift in the purposes teachers embrace and their active involvement in curriculum work (McLaughlin, 1997). It will require some measure of educational imagination to be exercised either through materials that are substantially developed by teachers or through teachers capably employing ready-made materials. There is, in other words, no choice but teachers thoughtfully tending the curricular-instructional gate if we want good education.

With the foregoing provisos in mind, what follows is an approach to curriculum planning in social studies. It is not presented as a comprehensive model but rather, as Ralph Tyler (1949) described the approach in his classic *Basic Principles of Curriculum and Instruction*, as methods "for studying" questions of the relationship of goals to curriculum planning (pp. 1–2). To this end, I analyze curriculum planning, especially as engaged in by teachers at the local level. It is an idealistic model that I recognize cannot be fully implemented on every occasion, given the press of circumstances under which many educators work. But the alternative to full use of a model need not be discarding it. The model should be broad enough to accommodate a variety of conceptions of the proper purposes and form of a social studies curriculum. Indeed, I expect that different educators will gravitate to different balances among the four types of goals suggested, as educational settings, needs, and aspirations properly vary. I hope, in any case, that educators will at least consider each of the four types of goals included, as each has commended itself to thoughtful educators.

Based on an analysis of the fundamental purposes Americans have held for public education over the long haul, John Goodlad (1994) identified the four types of goals that schools are asked or expected to address. This highly useful typology suggests that these goals are neither transitory nor shallow. Different goals have, though, had priority at different times and the content of some of them has shifted over time. Specifically, Goodlad suggested that the four categories are

> 1) academic—early emphasis was on sufficient schooling to learn the principles of religion and the laws of the land (sometimes defined as functional literacy); 2) vocational—readiness for productive work and economic responsibility; 3) social and civic—socialization for participation in a complex society; 4) personal—the goal of personal fulfillment, which is a fairly recent development. (pp. 43–44)

Significantly, each type of goal has seldom been a discrete entity in American popular education (see Cremin, 1990). For example, aims and goals in social studies such as history, geography, and civics reflected the conscious building of an American civic culture as much or more than the supposed academic benefits of these subjects for the general population (Elson, 1964; Morcau, 2003).

CONNECTIONS BETWEEN GOALS AND SUBJECT MATTER

Academic rationales for social studies subjects did, of course, exist in 19th-century American public schools, but aside from college preparation, they seem to have been less significant than what Goodlad (1994) called functional literacy. It is in this sense that the 1890s committees discussed in Chapters 1 and 2 were traversing relatively new territory when they suggested the academic study of subjects such as history for all students in the public schools. Even here, however, we should nonetheless be skeptical about claims that history was then being advocated for its own sake, as these committees invariably made a variety of other claims for the benefits of such study for general education, especially its role as a vehicle for citizenship education (Levstik, 1996; Rothstein, 2004; Watras, 2004).

Curriculum development, however, is more than a list of significant ideas, honored texts, social ideals, and so on. A curriculum must also transform images and aspirations about education into a series of activities in which students will engage (see Eisner, 2002, p. 126). As examined in Chapter 2, subject matter must be organized in some fashion and placed in some type of sequence, and directions must be given or implied for activities in which students will engage. Moreover, the nature of the learning process, including what young people are capable of or interested in learning and how they can be effectively engaged in learning it, inevitably helps shape the content eventually selected for inclusion in school programs. Moreover, in addition to what social scientists deemed suitable scholarship for study, questions of relevance to social-civic values have always played a part in what academic material is selected. These days, for example, study of 20th-century history includes the Holocaust in part, at least, as it is thought to convey important lessons about prejudice, intolerance, violence, and racism (see Fine, 1995); and geographic content is used to promote internationalism in student thinking and attitudes (see Marsden, 2000). Furthermore, as early as NEA's 1916 committee, it was recommended that subject matter selection be based on its current interest to the lives of students, in recognition that personal relevance greatly facilitates the educative effects of study.

Except, perhaps, for the opportunities rightly provided for deeply interested students and the demands of college preparation, the social sciences as understood in higher education have always been modified for the schools. Although academicians periodically decry such modifications, there is nothing intrinsically wrong with such an approach. Indeed, it is unavoidable: There is nothing within the social sciences that says which parts of them young people ought to study. These are educational rather than disciplinary questions, and educational criteria must be brought to bear to select what out of the universe of material in the social sciences should be included in school curricula, as the Committee on American History's report (Wesley, 1944) during World War II well illustrates (see Chapter 2).

Like social science goals, vocational goals suggest possible subject matters for the curriculum. But also like the social sciences, vocational purposes such as readiness for productive work and economic responsibility present the educator with a practically unbounded body of subject matter. Common usage in the United States associates vocational education with specific preparation for particular occupations in the adult world. In this sense, vocational purposes have played a limited but not inconsequential role in social studies curricula. During the early 20th century, for example, courses such as "commercial geography" were thought to be suitable preparation for the world of work, and although career guidance has generally been judged to be outside the legitimate scope of social studies, it was sometimes suggested that business education should be included (Marsden, 2001, p. 19).

If we construe vocational education more broadly than as preparation for actual occupations, however, curriculum theorists have envisaged a more central place for it in social studies. Dewey (1966), for instance, thought that schools preparing the young with the skills for particular occupations in the manner of trade schools would easily become out of date and be merely technical rather than reflective (p. 316). But this certainly did not mean that he believed that occupations were unimportant in school programs. To the contrary, he thought they should be the basis of the elementary-school curriculum. Insofar as it is possible to isolate what Dewey (1969) saw as the social studies part of occupations of the curriculum as a whole, he was expansive about the educational possibilities. What he (1990) wrote of geography spilled over into history and politics as well as much else of what he saw as the life relevance of the curriculum:

> The significance of geography is that it presents the earth as the enduring home of the occupations of man....It is through occupations determined by this environment that mankind has made its historical and political progress....In educational terms, this means that these occupations shall not be mere practical devices or modes of routine employment, the gaining of better technical skills as

cooks, seamstresses, or carpenters, but active centers of scientific insight into natural materials and processes, points of departure whence children shall be led out into realization of the historical development of man. (pp. 18–19)

Having said not much in the preceding discussion of academic aims that is explicitly about the intellect and the curriculum, I believe that it is worth adding that Dewey would have seen this, too, as an occupation. Students who have a deep, intellectual interest in a subject, say, geography, may experience joy in it as an occupation, and later perhaps will find themselves a career as a cultural geographer, meteorologist, climatologist, demographer, cartographer, environmentalist, or schoolteacher of geography. But even if it does not lead to a career, in addition to its offering the intrinsic satisfactions of geographic study and general education benefits, perhaps it might produce a lifelong interest in preserving nature or foreign travel or climatic calamities. Schools should, of course, value the intellectual occupation, but it is a mistake to force this on all students. As I have suggested earlier in this book, the genuine pursuit of the intellect as an occupation must be voluntary in a field the student wants to explore. Moreover, these interests Noddings (2003a) observes may arise in any field and are not restricted to "particular subjects or to superior mental capacities" (p. 216).

Vocational goals have also turned up in other forms over the history of the social studies. Even seemingly remote material such as ancient and medieval history has been deemed vocationally relevant. For example, the pertinence of medieval craft guilds to contemporary working and commercial conditions was noted by the first national report on social studies in 1916 (NEA, 1994, pp. 44–45). At the other end of the 20th century, a curriculum-reform project suggested goals for students' study of social roles (Superka & Hawke, 1982). These included providing awareness of careers directly related to the social sciences, helping reflection on worker-related experiences, providing knowledge to place in perspective the role of the worker in U.S. society and the world, and analysis and discussion of the interrelationships between the worker's role and other social roles such as those that citizens and family members of students assume (p. 120).

It is worth pausing here to observe that generally social-civic and personal-relevance criteria are used to select from the practically unbounded bodies of academic and vocational subject matter (see along the bottom of Figure 4.1). For example, what should the curriculum include in a study of the New Deal? If we consider social studies to be about "people—their individual rights and privileges, their adjustment to each other and to their world, and their working out of mutual problems" (Berger & Winters, 1973, p. 3), this definition suggests social-civic and personal goals. We then have some criteria by which to select which aspects of the New Deal to study—perhaps mutual problems such as low prices for farmers at the same time as food shortages in cities, or the rights of individual property versus the state's need to regulate the economy for the common good.

Alternately, academic and vocational subject matter is ordinarily required to provide a tangible way for teaching toward social-civic and personal-relevance goals. As noted, Dewey (1966) argued geography and history supply "the more direct and personal contacts of life" with "their context, their background and outlook" (p. 211). For instance, adolescents often express keen interest in their possessing basic rights, but they may be less interested in how individual rights can be reconciled with group needs in a liberal democracy. Here information about why affirmative action policies were conceived could provide background and outlook for an informed class discussion.

Although there are familiar exceptions such as the functions of government, social-civic goals do not always point to a particular body of content. Moreover, some of the most important social and civic goals probably cannot be directly taught. These goals might include attitudes about human rights, tolerance, justice, civic responsibility, and caring. We hope that such ideas will be learned through standard social studies topics (Thornton, 2002). Nonetheless, as my discussion of the Problems of Democracy course in Chapter 2 suggests, educators sometimes have a hard time deciding what subject matter is implied by social-civic purposes. Dissonance in this area between announced aims and subject matter selection is a long-standing problem in practice. For instance, the subject of civics was invented to address civic decision-making beyond the schoolhouse door and fails in its mission if it is, as is common, reduced to a repository of academic information drawn from political science (Dewey, 1991a).

Consider a further commonly expressed goal of social-civic education, "appreciation of global interdependence." This goal's most practicable enactment is probably in standard courses such as economics or world regions or global history (Thornton, in press). World trade is a likely topic by which the goal could be addressed. One method of introducing interdependence might be through discussion of current developments in the "globaliza- tion" of national economies. Almost certainly, however, we would want to employ organized bodies of knowledge such as geography and economics and their modes of inquiry to bolster and deepen such a discussion: How does trade connect world economies? To what extent is this phenomenon distributed uni- formly across the face of the planet? To what extent does global- ization make nations interdependent? How dependent is prosper- ity in the United States on economic developments in other countries? How much control does the United States have over multinational corporations? Does the United States owe special obligations to our largest trading partner, Canada, whose prosper- ity rests disproportionately on U.S. decisions?

Personal-fulfillment goals, as with social-civic goals, are often approached through academic and vocational subject matter. Scholarship itself, however, is seldom specifically designed to be relevant to the aptitudes and interests of a particular young per- son, despite such relevance being a common educational goal. Moreover, individual variation in what subject matter students find relevant is predictable and poses a pedagogical challenge: What if a student's chosen topic lacks substance, direction, or both? In this regard, Dewey (1963) went to some lengths to warn that the connection of subject matter to personal experience should not come at the price of "advance made in conscious artic- ulation of facts and ideas" (p. 75). But tension between freedom to choose subject matter and its leading somewhere that is educa- tionally significant appears to be built into a personal-fulfillment (or -relevance) approach. Dewey had a solution for this tension: "the participation of the learner in the formation of the purposes which direct his activities in the learning process" (p. 67). Teacher-pupil planning, he insisted, was essential for coherence in an individualized course of study.

With conditions being what they are in today's schools it is easy to dismiss teacher-pupil planning as unrealistic, given large class sizes, standards- and test-driven curricula, and other con- straints on teachers. Unlimited choice for students may not be possible in many circumstances, but must the alternative be no choice? Even under the most unfettered, ideal conditions, after all, teacher time, energy, imagination, and available materials still limit choice. Concomitantly, even the most conventional academic material provides some latitude for choice.

Consider a geography unit on the cultural landscape of Germany. Although there may be essential material, such as Germany's economic might, that all students will encounter, this does not mean that there cannot also be some room in the unit for personal interest. Perhaps these "interests" will not be a perfect match for each student, but limited choices will provide more opportunities for personal relevance than no opportunities or a reliance on the coincidence of student interest and the prescribed topics. Even limited choices can foster special interest on the part of the student. Indeed, allowing diverse approaches to a common topic can reveal connections between the topic and students' interests that they had previously not realized.

There are many possible topics broad enough to secure more general understandings about Germany, such as ethnic minorities, music or painting, youth culture or sports, urban architecture or transport, and relationships with neighboring countries. Such topics pursued in some depth forge connections with other salient features of German life (Whitehead, 1929). A properly guided project on ethnic minorities, for instance, will surely lead to investigation of Germany's post–Cold War borders, the economic factors that attracted "guest workers" from Turkey and other lands, tensions between immigrants and natives in regions of economic dislocation such as eastern Germany, and so on.

If significant material is missed, the teacher can still ensure that a representative and balanced treatment of the German cultural landscape is presented through a supplementary lecture or video or through small-group work. An additional benefit of the approach I am outlining is that students can be exposed to a wider set of perspectives on the topic than would be possible with the entire class studying the same material at the same pace.

These methods, here illustrated by German geography, remain controversial. Concern is often expressed that these methods will be lacking in substance. With careful planning, however, this need not be the case. The rule of thumb might be that goals should be viewed as being achievable through a variety of subject matters. And through use of a particular body of subject matter we might satisfy a variety of goals. Generally the curriculum should be regarded as an instrument to be manipulated by active educators rather than as an inflexible plan that confines them and forbids

Figure 4.1. Connections Between Goals and Subject Matter

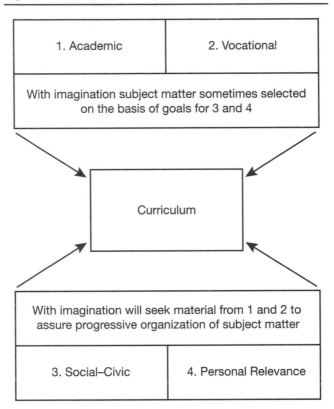

receptivity to individual differences in interests and aptitudes among students.

Thus far, I have argued that curriculum planners should strive for balance in the types of goals they suggest. Flexibility and balance seem most likely to be secured if goals and subject matter are simultaneously thought of rather than approached as distinct entities in a fixed relationship. Rather than goals being considered as tied to a particular body of subject matter and vice versa, there seems no good reason why these ties shouldn't be fluid and responsive to shifting purposes and emerging interests. As I will now take up, however, flexibility and balance will be to scant avail unless we envisage an active relationship between teachers and the curriculum.

TEACHERS AND THE CURRICULUM

Curricular-instructional gatekeeping can be one of the most rewarding challenges of teaching. It is moral intellectual work insofar as it relates to the teacher's capacity for knowledge and understanding as well as concern for students flourishing. This work involves the scholarship of the academy, but not that alone (Dewey, 1966). Teachers must take into account both the subject matter *and* "its interaction with the pupils' present needs and capacities." Dewey went so far as to say that scholarship "get[s] in the way of effective teaching" if divorced from "its interplay in the pupil's own experience" (p. 183).

Substantial teacher engagement with the curriculum—versus conceiving teachers as passive curriculum conduits—provides one of the profession's greatest satisfactions. This work is simultaneously academic and professional. Educational purposes and subject matter intermingle. For instance, purposes shift as fresh subject matter that looks richer and more promising emerges during instructional interactions. By the same token, other subject matter may be modified, perhaps discarded, as new and more powerful purposes arise.

Here we can see why it is a mistake to draw a sharp separation between educational purposes and teaching methods rather than regarding them as fluid and interdependent. David Snedden (1935), an early 20th-century proponent of educational efficiency previously mentioned, for instance, was surely wrong when he wrote:

> In other words, professional teachers...are...responsible for their employment of adequate *methods* of teaching, that is, of insuring desired learnings but not for the *purposes*, values of significances of such learnings. Only specialized policy-makers for educative processes...can effectively perform those other functions. (p. 10)

A divorce between purpose and method is untenable from the perspectives of both logic and experience. Policy makers nevertheless often behave as if this divorce were possible, even desirable. Policies resulting from such a perspective can curtail one of the most fertile opportunities for professional growth and satisfaction among teachers.

Snedden's error seems to be compounded when teachers engage in formal curriculum-development activities. Purposing is inherent in the very act of subject matter selection. Without purposing, we could never decide to include one thing rather than another. Indeed, studies of how curriculum-development teams proceed (versus idealized models of how they are supposed to proceed) reveal that actually creating materials requires building a "deliberative platform" of shared knowledge and beliefs (Walker, 2003). This set of ideas, as in its root metaphor of the planks of a political party's platform, guides their deliberations (p. 237). In other words, some sense of shared purposes by curriculum planners is necessary for orderly deliberation on subject matter selection and associated activities.

Even if some teachers never engage in formal curriculum development, all teachers implement curriculum materials and, in doing so, make a determination of the purposes that they believe were intended and that they themselves think are significant (Connelly & Ben-Peretz, 1997). Here, too, purposing (albeit, perhaps with scant conscious thought) is at work. The inevitability of purposing suggests we should raise teachers' consciousness about it. Gail McCutcheon (1997) has gone so far as to suggest that curriculum materials should be designed "to engage teachers in deliberation rather than materials that assume teachers are a direct pipeline from the expert developer to students' minds" (p. 196).

Curriculum implementation, then, is potentially an important site for staff-development activities based on the scholarship (i.e., curriculum materials) most closely related to teachers' professional responsibilities (Thornton, 2004a, 2004b). But unlike those of academicians, the professional responsibilities of teachers rarely do, nor should, allow them to focus solely on scholarly material (see Noddings, 2003b). To be sure, during implementation, teachers probably will (and certainly ought to) review the major concepts, principles, and skills embedded in the curriculum materials. This can be an important source of intellectual satisfaction. But teachers cannot stop there; they must also evaluate how the materials are sequenced, their difficulty level, their potential connections to student aptitudes and interests, their lateral connections to other important topics in the curriculum, gaps in the materials that may confuse students, what supplementary materials might be needed, and so on, as a basis for method, the effective direction of subject matter to desired results.

Despite the satisfaction that can be gained from the intellectual work of teaching, teachers vary in their responses to it and their abilities to do it (see Grant, 2003). Perhaps this should not be surprising. As noted, Harold Rugg (1936) argued that it is simply unrealistic to expect teachers to create a full-blown curriculum that is coherent and current, as the other demands on their time and imagination are too great. Reliance on what he called "spontaneous" curriculum making is a guarantee for chaos (p. 345). While his concern has a basis in experience, it does not follow that teachers ought to forsake all roles in curriculum development. Both curriculum and instruction can be strengthened by teachers having a significant stake in either creating or modifying a curriculum (Walker, 2003, pp. 294–295). The best teaching often stems from a curriculum that teachers have largely created themselves. The kind of carefully crafted curricula that Rugg developed for others to adapt and implement are doubtless needed in many cases, but we should take every opportunity to encourage able teachers in their own curriculum-development efforts (see Thornton, 1993).

CURRICULUM RECONSIDERED

The perspective I have been laying out in this chapter suggests rethinking the relationship between the teacher and the curriculum. I am not suggesting a utopian rethinking in which all curricular-instructional problems will be magically solved. To the contrary, I am proposing a challenging role for teachers. But it may also be a more satisfying and effective role than would be possible in conceiving of curriculum as something to be installed by teachers who lack significant agency. What might this look like?

Let us take a conventional geography topic to illustrate. To judge by widely used textbooks, in a treatment of the Eastern Hemisphere, Central Asia would probably only warrant a few lessons. Nevertheless, the teacher could arrange the curriculum so the purposes and subject matter are rich and important in this short curriculum sequence. In other words, the official curriculum needs to be interpreted, and possibly supplemented, in ways that avoid the customary criticism of geography instruction: an overreliance on the mere transmission of information such as in listing the chief rivers and major products, sketchily surveying climatic conditions, and locating national boundaries. In other words, the teacher should not present geography as a laundry list of locations, products, capitals, physical features, and the like.

An unrelated geographic-fragments curriculum so commonly arises, of course, for reasons rooted in the realities of schooling; how do we work around those obstacles? One such obstacle is likely to be standards. So an early planning task for the teacher is to work out how to address standards (which may well be tied to accompanying high-stakes tests) without contributing to curricular incoherence. An applicable set of standards in this case might be "environment and society," which includes knowing and understanding, for example, "how humans modify the physical environment" (Geography Education Standards Project, 1994, p. 35).

One topic to provide curricular focus might be the Aral Sea. This topic simultaneously incorporates the "environment and society" standards as well as supplying a theme, which can serve as an antidote to the subject matter becoming a hodgepodge. Given that Central Asia is an arid region, water is of particular significance economically, politically, diplomatically, and environmentally. In other words, it offers rich possibilities for exploring Central Asia from a variety of revealing perspectives. Teachers would want to choose which dimensions to cover depending on overall goals, student interests, current events, available curriculum materials, and so on.

"Water" is too broad a theme for just a few lessons. Hence it would make sense to select the Aral Sea as a hub for organizing study. This sea offers many fascinating and ominous dimensions for study. Once one of the world's great bodies of water, the fourth largest lake on the planet, in recent decades it has shrunk catastrophically in area and volume. What were once ports now lie in the desert dozens of miles from the sea's shoreline. Salt and other windblown contaminants of the atmosphere from vast expanses of the dry seabed have caused degradation of the environment, climate change, human health problems on a massive scale, and, understandably, widespread despair. It is a tragedy of essentially unprecedented proportions. And it is humanmade.

For the social studies curriculum, the Aral Sea could be used to illustrate almost any significant point we would need to make about Central Asia in a general-education course. Numerous entry points for study present themselves. For example, the origins of the catastrophe could be sought in Soviet aspirations to develop cotton production in their rivalry with the West. (The shrinkage of the sea, which moderated the climate, has now reduced the growing season below the minimum number of days needed for cotton!) Shipping and fishing have been reduced to a small fraction of the activity of a generation or so back. Because control of the sea and its tributary rivers is now spread over several nations as a result of the demise of the Soviet Union, international cooperation among the succession states and the broader world community has been and is indispensable to mitigating the disaster that has been unfolding.

If ever a vivid, contemporary example of the fateful interdependence of environment and human activity were available, the Aral Sea is surely it. Can or should the feeder rivers whose waters have been diverted be returned to filling the sea? Will recent attempts at international cooperation to restore parts of the ecosystem be sustained (see Global Security, 2004; Weinthal, 2002)? What economic choices do the peoples of the region have and how much do they rely on water that otherwise would help restore the sea? What should be done about it? Could this happen again? Do Americans or Europeans or Russians have a significant stake in mending what can be mended? Are other environmental problems in the world, say, Lake Chad in the Sahel of Africa, heading toward the same fate as that of the Aral Sea? It is hard to believe that student imagination wouldn't be captured by this grand fiasco of human stewardship of their home, the earth.

Note in this curriculum discussion that the curiosity aroused among students may well extend to motivation to be concerned with, investigate, make decisions about, other environmental issues, near and far. Moreover, they will have encountered the intricate and complex set of interrelationships—economic, environmental, and ideological—that constitute real-world problems. It is just this kind of dynamic that Whitehead (1929) had in mind when he spoke of the "rhythm of education" that continuously moves from reaching some closure to issues raised while sowing the seeds and enthusiasm for new inquiries.

Note, also, that the Aral Sea topic presents many different subtopics, which would be equally valuable in educational terms, but allow for teachers, and perhaps students as well, to choose, adapt, move among, and modify the material. The curriculum, in other words, becomes an array of inviting possibilities rather than a straitjacket. In purposefully maneuvering himself or herself and students the teacher engages in the great satisfaction of curricular gatekeeping.

In this chapter I have shown that the line between curriculum and instruction in teacher gatekeeping is unclear. It is mainly distinguished by the scale of the decisions. Nevertheless, while teachers may be required to cover the topic of the Civil War in a U.S. history curriculum, as gatekeepers they often can arrange and teach the curriculum through more microlevel method decisions to suit themselves. As explored in the following chapter, method—in another way of looking at it—is an arena where the teacher ordinarily has greater autonomy than in deciding the form and content of the curriculum. This makes the quality of gatekeeping decisions and actions, and hence the curriculum students experience, matters that are largely determined by teachers once the classroom door is closed.

5 *Methods*

Probably no complaint about social studies is more familiar than that teaching methods fail to capture student interest. Instruction, young people say, can be dull and irrelevant to their lives. Students may like their teachers well enough and have definite interest in social questions, but young people perceive these factors as disconnected from the instruction they receive (Thornton, 1991).

While in Chapter 3 we investigated the sources of aims, and in Chapter 4 how goals and subject matter implied by those aims do (or ought to) function in curriculum planning, in this chapter I concentrate on method. In particular, method should reflect the aims and goals of the curriculum as well as suit the particular teaching situation. Otherwise, instruction will fail to realize its announced purposes (Thornton, 1988). The teacher's prime task is effective direction to desired results of the subject matter specified or implied in a curriculum.

CURRICULUM REFORM AND THE NEGLECT OF METHODS

There appears to be a long-standing prejudice on the part of educational reformers against what they have apparently seen as the mundane matter of method. Convinced that only subject matter is educationally worth talking about, reformers have generally been more intrigued by systematic curriculum development than classroom instruction (Harper, 1938; Hertzberg, 1988). Curricula are, however, but a point of departure for instruction. Herbert Kliebard (1979) defined systematic curriculum development as (1) why to teach one thing rather than another, (2) to whom it is taught and under what circumstances, (3) in what ways it should be taught, and (4) how the components of the curriculum are interrelated so that the sum of the whole equates with what it now means to be educated (pp. 202–203).

The prestigious individuals and groups who participate in systematic curriculum development, or at least put their names to the documents, suggests it is a high-status activity. The element of classroom method, what Kliebard called ways of teaching, is usually the part of systematic curriculum development least attended to. Although reformers are quick to concede that methods are integral to curriculum development, they frequently announce that attention to method is beyond their time and resources (e.g., Bradley Commission on History in Schools, 1988; National Commission on Social Studies in the Schools, 1989; Wesley, 1944).

Perhaps curriculum development holds greater allure than altering classroom methods because it creates the impression that relatively quick and decisive change is in the developer's hands. Method is idiosyncratic and slow, harder to systematize. Nevertheless, systematic curriculum development often fails to effect significant alterations in method (Shaver, 1979). If method is the chief problem of social studies, a charge repeated for more than a century, proposed solutions often appear to be misaligned with the problem. It is hard to escape the suspicion that many reformers expect alterations in method as a more or less automatic by-product of curriculum change. A comment by Fred Newmann (1985) reinforces this suspicion. Appraising more than 30 national reports on educational reform that appeared in the early 1980s, he observed that the reports were "remarkably unhelpful to teachers in social studies or other subjects." Further, he noted: "If a teacher were to ask of the reports, 'What can I do next week in my classes to stimulate more student excitement and commitment or learning?' he or she would find virtually no useful advice" (p. 23).

A curriculum is a series of activities intended to engage students in educational experiences, but it is necessarily cast in general terms, because instructional settings where it is enacted vary and cannot be entirely foreseen. A curriculum presents teachers with images and aspirations, not with a script. As the Problems of Democracy course in the decade following its 1916 conception shows, however, skeletal outlines of even enthusiastically rendered and quickly implemented products of systematic curriculum development can flounder in execution if they are too parsimonious about method. As noted in Chapter 2, teachers' demands for practicable methods eroded the interactive goals of the Problems of Democracy course, resulting in a course more akin to an introduction to academic political science.

Widespread implementation of innovative social studies curricula appears to be associated with change proposals that are sensitive to methods concerns (Hertzberg, 1981). Alternately, curricula that have neglected method frequently fail to find a secure place in school programs (p. 166). To reiterate, sensitivity does not translate into a teacher-proof script. Rather, it suggests that curriculum developers should devise materials rich enough to engage teachers in deliberation about the alternative possibilities that the materials present (McCutcheon, 1994).

Curriculum development is not, despite common usage, a unitary phenomenon. Decker Walker (1979) has argued that its meaning refers to at least three distinguishable enterprises, which may or may not overlap much: (1) curriculum policymaking, (2) generic curriculum development, and (3) site-specific curriculum development (pp. 268–276). Although considerations of method may arise in any of these enterprises, it is generally least considered in policymaking and most considered in site-specific work. This is scarcely surprising, as the closer one moves to the site where curriculum is enacted, the more its interconnections with method are likely to emerge during deliberation.

Curriculum policymaking establishes the limits, criteria, guidelines, and the like with which curricula must comply, without developing actual plans and materials for use by students and teachers (Walker, 1979, p. 269). In social studies, policymaking has been of two main kinds. The first comes from state laws and regulations. States have for generations mandated specific instruction in subjects such as American history, state history, and the federal and state constitution. Further, states commonly also shape curriculum policies through frameworks for courses to be offered, textbook adoption, and testing. Federal policies have increasingly impinged also in recent years, albeit usually indirectly, through means such as national content standards. As has been explored earlier, commissions have also played a historic role in formulating social studies curriculum policy, with varying degrees of legitimacy and influence. But both government and commissions have generally had little to say about method. American history may be required for certain grade levels or a particular number of minutes of instruction each week, and so on, but specific guidance on method such as with the Committee of Seven (AHA, 1899) is the exception rather than the rule. The 1916

Social Studies in Secondary Education (NEA, 1994) or the 1980s National Commission on Social Studies in the Schools (1989) are more typical in their scant treatment of method.

A second form of curriculum development is what Walker (1979) called generic curriculum development. That is the preparation of curriculum plans and materials for use potentially by any students or teachers of a given description. This form of curriculum development varies widely in the specificity of its treatment of method. As discussed earlier, the Rugg materials provided extraordinary guidance for method. However, curriculum plans in the form of state-issued syllabi or frameworks for a course can be spare about method. When New York State introduced a series of mandates moving from a regional world cultures organization called global studies to a chronologically organized world history and geography in the 1990s, for example, the state mandate said almost nothing about methods; however, educational leaders behaved as if methods would change (Grant, 2003, pp. 202–203).

The third form of systematic curriculum development is site specific. Probably most often this is the implementation of commercially produced curriculum materials, ensuring teacher comfort with and use of the materials. Sometimes districts or schools will appoint a curriculum committee to produce a curriculum plan based on the commercially produced materials. For example, at one site the tables of contents from the social studies textbook series adopted were slightly adapted to form a curriculum guide (Thornton & Wenger, 1990). Less commonly, more original and elaborate site-specific development occurs. One district on Long Island, New York, for instance, was initially motivated to create a required ninth-grade human relations course by swastikas appearing on a Jewish temple followed by vandalism of a church. The school district came to believe that existing social studies courses tended to be too directed to bias, intolerance, and hatred somewhere distant in time and space; therefore, this new course was developed and refined in the district over the course of several years. Much of the revision centered on aligning methods with the curriculum's locally oriented purposes (Libresco & Wolfe, 2003).

Whichever form curriculum development takes, however, clearly method and curriculum development are interdependent activities. It is customary to speak of curriculum development as the *what* of teaching, and method as the *how*. This dichotomy is neat but imprecise, because how we teach becomes part of what we teach and what we teach influences which methods we select.

It is nonetheless useful to distinguish curriculum from method, because the work of teachers is ordinarily at a more microscopic level than is systematic curriculum development. It is the methods teachers use that exploits one or more of a curriculum's potentials (Ben-Peretz, 1975).

FROM CURRICULUM TO METHOD

Neither curriculum nor method ever exist in the abstract; they are an organized body of materials about something or a way of arranging something for instruction, respectively. Actualization of either curriculum or method requires a transformation of subject matter guided explicitly or implicitly by educational purposes. It is in this educational transformation, only touched on so far, that we encounter a crucial distinction: between knowing a subject as scholarship and knowing how to organize it for purposes of instruction (Thornton, 2001b).

For example, a beginning teacher may "know" his or her college major of political science but still poorly grasp the content of a civics or participation in government course. The former is a body of scholarly concepts and principles, methods, and dispositions. The latter are school courses intended to develop young people's competence in and caring about political citizenship. Although the scopes of academic political science and civics or participation in government clearly overlap, just as clearly they are not identical (Hunt, 1935). It is in this sense that teacher educators have long been skeptical of the claim that a college major in a single academic subject adequately prepares a prospective teacher for the subject matter demands of even that subject (Smith, 1965, p. 31).

Imagine that a new teacher is assigned to teach a civics course. Although this particular teacher has never taken a social studies teaching-methods course, organization of a course will be expected. At minimum, the teacher will likely be given a syllabus-like curriculum and a textbook. The teacher may first try to reconcile the differences between the curriculum and the textbook in what topics they treat and what order the topics come in. The teacher's first planning task is to decide, at least preliminarily, what key topics and skills to cover and in what order.

Although our hypothetical beginning teacher did study political science in college, the political science professors organized those courses. Even if our teacher had been afforded opportunities to organize material in college seminars or independent studies, these methods may be unsuitable for teaching civics to children. The teacher needs to be able to arrange subject matter from a curriculum devised for immature learners as part of their general education. The curriculum is intended to develop competence in civic decision-making (Oliver & Shaver, 1966). This goal might be well served by methods such as problem solving or community study or the analysis of public policy. At any rate, our teacher, unschooled in method, is in a poor position to make an informed choice for any given setting even if he or she is familiar with methods beyond the academic.

In this sense of selecting appropriate methods, beginning teachers are often perplexed about how they should decide to employ one method rather than another. Some of them respond by doggedly following the teacher's guide to the textbook or some method that purports to deliver classroom control. Others fixate on a particular model or arbitrarily select models for the sake of "variety." Each of these responses is less than ideal in terms of method. Method is being confused with mere technique divorced from subject matter. It is a common error, Dewey (1991b) noted, for the educator to assume "that there is one set body of subject matter and of skills to be presented to the young, only requiring to be presented to and 'learned' by the child" (p. 240).

Let's assume another new teacher untrained in method has been assigned to teach a seventh-grade course on ancient and early medieval Western civilization. He has a textbook that covers the intended scope and sequence of the course. His department chairperson tells him he has considerable discretion over the emphases for the course—as long, however, as our new teacher deals with all the skills seventh-graders are supposed to master. The subject matter is conventional; in fact it is much the same content this teacher had encountered in the seventh grade. The main topics listed are early humans, the rise of river valley civilizations in Egypt and Mesopotamia, ancient Greece and Rome, the development of Christianity and Islam, the Byzantine Empire, feudal Europe. Skills in interpreting primary sources, reading various kinds of maps, researching from various places such as the internet, and writing short essays are also specified.

The teacher's first response to this material is to consider what he knows about it. He recalls his college coursework. Lectures on Periclean Athens, Greek art, Roman imperialism, and the origins of feudalism and Christianity come to mind. He retrieves from an old file a term paper he had prepared on the decline of the Roman Empire. His memories of college work on medieval Europe are foggier, and he studied nothing that he can recall on the rise of Islam or the Byzantine Empire. Nevertheless, the teacher concludes that he knows enough on most of the topics to come up with a preliminary arrangement of topics with emphases on the areas he is most familiar with. But he is far less confident specifically on how the material can be broken down and organized into lessons and what kinds of activities he and the students will engage in. Nor is it apparent where and when skills should be taught and whether they should be discrete lessons or taught in the context of a topic.

It is probably fair to say that some variant of this scenario typifies the experience of most beginning social studies teachers. Even if, unlike our hypothetical teachers, a new teacher has taken a social studies methods course, one course is a meager preparation for the pedagogical demands of subject matter. More likely the methods that come to mind will reflect the teacher's experiences in school and college, especially the most recent and hence best recalled of those experiences in college and high school. In an important sense, those experiences, with their reliance on instructor-directed lecture and discussion, outnumber by many times the more innovative methods to which the teacher may have been exposed. Years of socialization to methods that may be more familiar than effective stands a good chance of outweighing preparation in alternative methods.

In a methods course or two, the amount of valuable material that could be covered is completely out of proportion to the available time. Methods courses are typically designed as an introduction to the arrangement of material, skills, and accompanying curriculum materials. Competence in the pedagogical demands of the expansive school social studies curriculum is, however, a challenging task for the prospective secondary-school teacher. For example, she or he ought to have methods work in, among other subjects, U.S. history and government, global history and geography, economics, and current events (Thornton, 2001a).

PRINCIPLED SELECTION OF METHODS

If our new teacher did have sufficiently detailed work on methods for his seventh-grade course, what methods and materials might present themselves? In other words, what are some methods beyond college academics that might be suitable and what principles should guide their selection? It was in responding to these kinds of questions that Whitehead's (1929) notion of the rhythm of education is particularly important. To reiterate, he argued figuratively that instruction should be guided by what he referred to as the stages of romance, precision, and generalization. Whitehead thought the rhythm of education demanded romance, a stage of discovery and arousing curiosity, preceding the kind of precision or generalization in the academic model with which our beginning teachers are most familiar from college.

Romance might suggest for seventh-grade pupils a variety of methods and curriculum materials. Interest in Greek civilization might be spurred by a discovery lesson on the figures on an ancient vase. Feudalism may be best approached through making models of a medieval manor. Much of ancient Rome could be studied through its present-day ruins, and relevant photographs could readily be found in almost any course textbook or on the internet. Or perhaps the twilight of the Roman world and the birth of the Middle Ages would easily capture children's imaginations if they read engrossing historical fiction. For example, even a few words from the opening of Rosemary Sutcliff's (1994) *The Lantern Bearers* could usefully frame an important discussion of a disintegrating civilization. Take the protagonist of the novel. Upon his return to his family's estate in once orderly and prosperous Roman Britain, he observes: "And really, the place didn't look so bad. It was not what it had been in the good, old days, of course" (p. 3). But even if our teacher adopts any of these approaches, he may have done so without system in his thinking about method. Lacking principles to guide method, the teacher is unable to generalize from even lessons where the methods were highly effective.

A principled approach to method also requires careful reflection on not only what—why this rather than that?—but also on how much subject matter is taught. Whitehead (1929) observed in this regard that "the area of precise knowledge, as exacted in any general educational system, can be, and should be, definitely determined." Again, our young teacher likely lacks a sound criterion for making such decisions. "If you make it too wide you will kill interest and defeat your own object," Whitehead continued, but "if you make it too narrow your pupils will lack effective grip." Whitehead was once more pointing to sensitivity to the rhythm of education, here in content selection. There is, he maintained, "no simple formula" applicable to all students, in all subjects, at all times except the "formula of rhythmic sway" (p. 56).

Whitehead's conception of rhythm in education was cast in terms of the curriculum in general. Other educators have explored more subject-specific questions, including criteria for selecting appropriate methods within particular social studies such as current events, anthropology, or geography. In a once well-known methods book, for instance, five criteria were underscored: (1) the nature of the topic, (2) the needs of individuals and the group, (3) variety of methods to arouse interest, (4) a teacher's "style," and (5) balance among individual, small-group, and large-group experiences (Kentworthy, 1970, pp. 79–80).

These criteria have not been thoroughly explored by educational researchers. But some of the criteria such as the first—the nature of the topic—are consistent with research findings suggesting that the kinds of methods employed by seasoned educators vary with the nature of the subject for apparently sound reasons (Brophy, 2001; Stodolsky, 1988). As I suggest above, a passage from Sutcliff's *The Lantern Bearers* may be particularly suited to evoking the mood of an historical era in a way that direct instruction could fail to do. Similarly, I also noted that purposeless variety in method may reflect a more general aimlessness, even mindlessness, in instruction. It could also be, however, that variety deployed in a purposeful manner reawakens interest in a topic when repeated exposure through one method has grown stale (Kentworthy, 1970).

Almost certainly there is no one best method. Rather, we need to ask what method is well suited to this material with these students at this time in these circumstances. Conscious consideration of method in this way is a principled alternative to the mindlessness critics have charged too often characterizes subject matter and method selection in social studies. Following are demonstrations of different "types" of method. They are offered as suggestive types of purposeful educational deliberation rather than as algorithms to be followed. The types represented here fail, of course, to exhaust the range of possibilities.

Lesson Types

A narrow and sometimes monotonous range of methods has characterized social studies instruction (Goodlad, 1984). This situation will not be remedied by a panacea of the "right" method, as has been tried periodically; nor will it be solved by greater variety in methods for the sake of variety. What is needed is a principled and creative approach to methods selection. I should add at the outset that I am not participating in the hackneyed condemnation of "traditional" methods, such as lecture, as warranting blanket condemnation. In the right circumstances dominant methods devoted to knowledge transmission are entirely appropriate. There is a problem, however, when lecture (or anything else) is overused. I am arguing that most lessons in an instructional unit should feature some knowledge construction by students rather than complete reliance on someone else's completed act of thought.

While the lessons analyzed here are intended to elicit active engagement of students, such engagement does not replace dealing with substantial subject matter—it enhances it (White, 1986). A common barrier to the improvement of method seems to be the suspicion that attention to process comes at the expense of significant content and vice versa. To the contrary, the most effective learning of content stems from engaging methods. Lest this is considered a truism, it should be recalled that there is a long history of educational critics contending that process comes at the *expense* of substantial subject matter (Thornton, 2001c).

By the same token, Dewey (1963) was also right that educational worth does not inhere in pieces of subject matter (p. 46). Although he did not deny that some subject matter held greater educational potential than other subject matter, at the same time Dewey insisted that, say, neither the Renaissance nor team sports was intrinsically more valuable as subject matter. All depended on how they were studied. The Renaissance could be dealt with superficially or misleadingly; and sports, if thoroughly explored, could lead to student engrossment in substantial subject matter.

For instance, in a study of India, students would encounter the long Indian struggle to expel the British imperialists and at the same time confront the fact that "British" customs, such as the sport of cricket, have endured into the "postcolonial" era.

The first type of method I shall deal with, like the Indian cricket illustration, shows how, with the right approach, a rich tapestry of student knowledge and hypotheses can emerge from what might appear academically unpromising subject matter. Consider a unit on the Roman Empire. An introduction to the unit might take the form of a teacher-led inductive lesson with a photograph of a Roman arch. Discovery (or inquiry) learning is utilized in this method; the teacher and the students mutually construct a tentative characterization of Roman civilization.

The lesson begins with the whole class looking at a photograph of a Roman arch. The students are told that, even though they are just beginning their study of Roman civilization, they may already know a good deal about it. Student comments are invited. Someone observes that, as it is a photograph, the arch has endured for a long time, since the ancient Roman Empire did not have photography. This leads to comments about how the Romans must have been fairly accomplished builders for the arch to last so long in apparently decent condition. Other students suggest that they have seen movies of Roman ruins and perhaps the Romans were good engineers and architects. The discussion takes a different turn when a student comments on the etchings on the monument: Who would pay for such an arch and what were the etchings for?

The discussion grows more speculative. Some students add that the arch could be a memorial to someone important, perhaps a military figure, like Grant's Tomb in New York City. Why else build such a structure? Who would go to the trouble? Would, for example, women have played any role in conceiving or building the arch if it commemorated victory in war? What kind of society values its history enough to commemorate it? A student excitedly declares, "Rome must have had money" because the arch serves no apparent practical function—this was a society wealthy enough to pay for luxuries.

The teacher now tries to assemble the ideas that have arisen and lead the student observations and hypotheses toward important themes to be developed in the Rome unit. She points out that the Romans were good engineers and architects. She shows pictures of roads, aqueducts, and the Coliseum of Rome. The teacher and students organize themselves for further inquiry by framing questions on what the roads might have been used for—trade and moving troops are suggested, but it is agreed that research will be needed to confirm these hunches. Similarly, the class agrees that investigation will be needed about aqueducts: Did they deliver water to towns, farms, or both? Who constructed them and who footed the bill? The discussion continues along these lines for several more minutes, but significantly, curiosity has been aroused and arrangements are made to divide up research work through seatwork or individual or group projects. The students seem confident, it is worth noting, that they already have a foundation of knowledge and hypotheses to build upon rather than starting from scratch.

This type of lesson illustrates the possibilities of teacher-led inquiry. The teachers' role here is primarily to stimulate and direct student curiosity. Moreover, it may be that concern that there is insufficient time for inquiry lessons with today's overcrowded curriculum is overstated. As the foregoing lesson description suggests, inquiry can be both a productive and an *efficient* use of scarce instructional time. I am reminded here, as an example, of a sixth-grade textbook on world regions with a large, striking photograph of a ship marooned high and dry on what had once been the bottom of the Aral Sea (*World Regions*, 2003). Such a photograph could easily stimulate a lively lesson for a whole class period or more. It is also worth noting that rich collections of curriculum materials and activities suitable for discovery episodes— or closely related constructivist methods—still exist from the New Social Studies projects (e.g., Beyer, 1994).

The decision of when to employ discovery (or constructivist, for that matter) methods usually rests on the nature of the subject matter. There must be something you can reasonably expect that can be discovered. It is a stretch, for instance, to "discover" the names of the federal agencies established by the New Deal (although even here a creative teacher might have a shot at it, asking, "What problems did Franklin Roosevelt confront and, by deduction, what kinds of agencies were needed?"). In creating the instructional arrangements for an act of discovery, usually we look for a topic that does not require new skills or information but just the steady application, reformulation, or synthesis of material already in hand; or, as with the Rome example above, we look for material from which a conclusion can be drawn inductively.

Discovery methods can be especially powerful, but they can also be time-consuming and will probably not be used in every lesson. Again, we are reminded here not to fixate on one "best" method. But even used sparingly, discovery lessons can be intrinsically worthwhile as well as profitably flow over into the rest of an instructional unit or course. On this point, Lee Cronbach (1966) wrote:

> When I propose that some small fraction of the course use discovery methods, I am not saying "and let the rest of the course remain as it was." On the contrary, I want didactic teaching modified to capitalize on the meanings and attitudes that were established through discovery. (p. 87)

In contrast to discovery, a second type of method, small-group work, can be suitable for almost any subject matter, depending on your purposes. The decision to employ small-group methods normally depends on factors such as the amount of self-direction and cooperation the teacher wants students to experience and a relatively low expectation of uniform outcomes (Noddings, 1989). Small groups can also be handy for dividing up large topics, which might otherwise be unmanageable in the available instructional time, by forming specialist groups. These large topics may be "postholes," which is pausing in a survey course to examine a selected topic in some depth, such as in a detailed treatment of the woman suffrage movement in a survey course in American history.

Alternatively, a large topic may be subdivided by highlighting a selected theme in it. The theme should throw into relief an idea that significantly modifies our understanding of a topic. In a unit on the development of the American West, for example, we could introduce the generalization that the region is characterized by scarcity of water as a theme. The theme draws together otherwise disparate threads of the topic. Thus, without the extensive detour from a survey possibly required by postholing, our theme underscores, for instance, the significant connections between topics such as water supply for the arid Los Angeles basin, competing interstate and international (with Mexico) claims on the Colorado River, and the economic and environmental dimensions of the massive irrigation scheme in California's Central Valley. It seems that even though "we forget the details," we "remember the impression that the details made upon us" (Engle & Longstreet, 1972). In this sense, themes are the "education" that "stays in our mind after the specifics of what we have learned have been forgotten" (p. 16).

Thematic work with groups enables broad treatment of a topic such as the American West without superficiality. Or another possibility would be again establishing specialist groups and assigning each of the subtopics mentioned above to a separate group, later the whole class coming together to share what has been learned.

A third type of lesson, which could be discovery or group work or didactic, is the development of a central concept. The centerpiece of this third type of lesson is perhaps most usefully called a "big idea" (White, 1988). Big ideas should be "sufficiently simple so that students can understand them, yet sufficiently complex so that grasping the concept helps to reorganize the students' understanding of what they have previously learned" (p. 122). Rather than start with particulars and move toward a generalization, as in the inductive lesson above, this type of lesson would start with a big idea and then develop it. There are available good analyses of how this type of lesson could unfold, such as developing the concept of imperialism (Illinois Curriculum Program, 1971) or teaching for understanding with the Fall Line (White & Rumsey, 1993).

For example, the big idea could be "desertification." In a unit on Africa, this idea could be introduced and used to forge new connections and understandings in the subject matter, for instance, in studying the impoverished Sahel region, a band of arid grassland that runs east-west along the southern edge of the Sahara Desert. In recent decades the Sahel has shifted to the south. This appears to be part of a natural cycle of increased aridity (Pulsipher, 1999).

The desertification of these fragile grasslands, however, has probably been hastened or worsened by human modifications to the environment such as overgrazing of domesticated animals or clearing and plowing marginal land for agriculture. The loss of topsoil results in its replacement by sand (pp. 344–345). In any case, a variety of physical and human processes could be examined in a study of desertification and possible ways of mitigation of the process explored.

Big ideas, like the aforementioned highlighting, tend to be remembered. Nonetheless, the number of big ideas in a lesson, unit, or course should be limited, as their advantage for recall will be squandered if there are too many of them. Big ideas are also powerful because they can transfer to new subject matter. For example, one manifestation of the southward shift of the Sahel is the shrinkage of the once vast Lake Chad since the mid-20th century. If the same class had studied the Aral Sea, the idea of the shrinkage of bodies of water and its natural and human causes could be compared and contrasted with the phenomena concerning Lake Chad.

CONCLUSION

My analysis of method in this chapter implies the need for effective teachers to possess both rich knowledge of subject matter and the ability to adjust purposes with the curriculum and method. These two requisites are, however, staple criticisms of social studies teaching by subject matter authorities and supervisors of classroom teaching, respectively. But perhaps the characteristic separate origin of these two criticisms is itself revealing. Teachers and students never encounter subject matter and method as separate from each other.

From this perspective, there may be an inherent flaw in attempts to improve instruction through teacher education based on sharp separation of subject matter and method. Teachers don't need just "more" subject matter knowledge, but a kind suitable for the pedagogical demands of the curriculum; by the same token, competence in method cannot be fully developed separate from purposes for the arrangement of particular subject matter for a particular educational setting.

In the following chapter, I consider the challenges that this interdependence of subject matter and method poses for teacher education. Although I'll suggest some fundamental changes in the education of social studies teachers, I'll also argue that much of what I suggest could be incrementally incorporated under existing institutional arrangements for teacher education. In other words, making teacher education programs more relevant to the actual demands of teaching need not adhere to the frequently destructive principle of "all or nothing." We could wait forever for comprehensive reforms such as restructured schools or nationally board-certified teachers. Meanwhile the enterprise of teacher education continues—the next chapter is written with this fact in mind.

6

Educating the Educators

How should teachers be prepared to tend the curricular-instructional gate? What do teachers need to know about the social sciences and related material not emanating from the traditional academic subjects, such as current events, in order to teach social studies? Who should answer this question? What preparation and support should teachers have to marshal the subject matters of the curriculum for instruction?

The answers to these questions are contested for the enterprise of teacher education as a whole. To the extent possible, this chapter is restricted to answering the aforementioned questions for the exclusively *social studies* element of teacher preparation in pre- and in-service education: social science and related subject matter and method. Although general education, educational foundations, and student teaching are also normally part of teacher preparation programs—and may significantly shape the character of preparation in social studies—I leave systematic treatment of those concerns common to all subject areas to others (e.g., Armento, 1996; Hiebert, Gallimore, & Stigler, 2002).

How one proposes to prepare social studies teachers rests, whether recognized or not, on some conception of the field's proper purposes and the models of curriculum and of instruction they imply. Whatever these purposes are construed to be, however, teacher education programs must connect in some manner to preparation for teaching the modal American social studies curriculum. This curriculum, as noted in earlier chapters, is an amalgam of courses that are either essentially simplifications of the social sciences in higher education, which are customarily assumed as a by-product to cultivate good citizenship, or social education courses, which are nonetheless supposed to be informed by social science scholarship.

In either case, any reasonable person would have to acknowledge that even the most circumscribed social studies curriculum is practically unbounded in the subject matter demands it places on teachers. No one is, or could be, an authority on all of American history and government, the geography and cultures of the entire contemporary world, micro-, macro-, and consumer-economics, the history of every major civilization on the globe from early humans to the present, and so on. Yet even this fails to exhaust the scope of the curriculum. In other words, when policymakers such as Secretary of Education Rod Paige propose that "teachers should be trained in the subjects they teach" such as "history" (Paige, 2001), they may provoke the comment that even a history major seldom prepares teachers for the entire range of *history* topics in the school curriculum, let alone the other social studies (Smith, 1965; Thornton, 2001a).

In the remainder of this chapter I will first turn to subject matter preparation. I consider both the state of current practices and a variety of possible alternative courses of action—all of which imply closer alignment of subject matter and method preparation in higher education with the subject matter and method demands of the school curriculum. Then, at somewhat greater length, I look at the most direct means of teacher education available: the social studies methods course. I explore both common criticisms of the course and suggest possibilities for making it a more effective instrument of teacher education. Here, too, I suggest we would profit by better aligning subject matter and method preparation. Finally, I selectively examine some possible alternative emphases in staff development or in-service education.

SUBJECT-MATTER PREPARATION

It is worth beginning this section by observing that most of the coursework in teacher education programs takes place in arts and sciences courses, not education courses. Seldom, however, do social science professors appear to consider which parts of their subject specialties may be relevant to the subject matter needs of school teachers (Ochoa, 1981). Indeed, strangely enough, few professors in any of the arts or sciences ever seem to consider that they are teacher educators (Griffin, 1999). This neglect of the needs of teachers can be compounded by lack of or ineffective communication between arts and sciences faculty and education school faculty.

Subject matter and method were not always isolated from each other in teacher education programs. In the old teachers' colleges, which largely disappeared in the mid-20th century, there was a union of subject matter and method. For all these colleges' shortcomings, such as their being unlikely to attract top-drawer liberal arts faculty, teacher education was an institutional mission in contrast to the piecemeal treatment teacher education typically receives in today's colleges and universities. Students who were preparing to teach social studies took social science courses, but these courses were so constructed that methods were interwoven with the new subject matter (Noddings, 1998a). Lecture courses in the social sciences could explore themes useful in teaching the school curriculum. For example, a series of lectures might focus on the theme of human migration over time, perhaps looking at Germanic tribes, the Vikings, and the Mongols, as well as mass migration in modern times.

Furthermore, it was more likely than in social science courses in today's colleges and universities that a geography or history professor had, perhaps even still did, regularly taught children. Perhaps these professors would offer "demonstration" lessons. In any case, the art and craft of teaching were embedded in their courses, whereas in universities such craft knowledge holds lower status than research activity (Cuban, 1999; Herbst, 1989; Weiler, 1999).

Since roughly the mid-20th century, also, institutional arrangements in universities have not prioritized the general or professional dimensions of undergraduate courses (Silberman, 1970). The decline of liberal arts faculty commitment to general education has resulted in fewer available courses relevant to the synthetic demands of school curriculum and teaching method; it has also helped draw social scientists away from involvement in writing original textbooks, constructing primary-source anthologies, and preparing other curriculum materials for the schools (Hertzberg, 1988). Understandably in a culture where research is rewarded far more than teaching, social science professors gravitate to courses in their own specialties. For example, as one prospective teacher told me, she enrolled in an undergraduate geography course anticipating its suitability for teachers only to find the instructor's focus on Foucault dimly, if at all, connected to the content of the school curriculum.

Of course, there are alternatives to social science departments and departments and schools of education ignoring one another. Perhaps the most likely impetus for such a move would come from social studies education professors conferring with their social science colleagues about which standard courses already offered might best mesh with the school curriculum. In my own experience, for example, a geography department welcomed the opportunity to serve elementary education majors' needs with a world geography course. If told, for example, that geography in elementary and secondary education should be guided by, say, Dewey's (1966) definition of its significance in general education—"an account of the earth as the home of man" (p. 211)—what might geographers be inspired to come up with?

Sometimes more formalized collaborations are undertaken. These seem particularly needed in the preparation of elementary teachers who take just a few courses in the social sciences (and those courses will probably bear no planned relationship to one another) thus often relegating the main job of teaching relevant subject matter to already overburdened methods courses. One possible remedy for this situation has been tried at the University of Delaware. The science courses required of elementary education majors treated content that would form the basis of the elementary school science-methods course. Prospective teachers, in other words, studied topics such as the ecology of the Delaware Bay that they would be expected to arrange for instructional purposes in their methods course (Madsen et al., 2001). Even when successful, however, this type of cross-campus collaboration apparently consumes greater time and effort than either liberal arts or education professors are accustomed to expending (Brickhouse, 2003). Moreover, often when the special funding runs out, so does the innovation. These stumbling blocks once again suggest that universities may need to reexamine existing resource allocations if they are serious about institutional commitment to teacher education.

Although sometimes characterized by indifference or acrimony, collaboration in teacher education can enliven the professional lives of both social scientists and social studies methods instructors. One of the few available case studies documents such collaboration. It brought together university social studies methods instructors and social scientists (as well as experienced teachers) in a shared teaching of the social studies methods course (McKee & Day, 1992). This use of a multiple-stakeholder participation in the methods course proved to be instructionally effective. Moreover, it energized the instructors. For example, a history professor concluded: "I more fully realize the need for modeling in arts and sciences a variety in both method and content. I also see a need for liberal arts instructors to make assignments that are more closely linked to the career goals of education majors" (cited in McKee & Day, 1992, p. 184).

Sadly, such hopeful signs seem exceptional. It is disheartening to recall that for decades reformers have called for academic courses to integrate the social sciences around themes that could drive a dynamic social studies curriculum (e.g., Smith & Cox, 1969, pp. 158–159; Sosniak, 1999, pp. 190–192; Wesley, 1944, p. 107). Even secondary-school teachers who likely major in a particular social science—a practice routinely extolled by conservative policymakers and academicians alike as a veritable cure-all for teacher education, incidentally—may still be inadequately prepared. Study of a single social science (or two of them if the prospective teacher minors in a second social science) may still be scant preparation for the lateral connections across the social sciences, humanities, and "science, technology and society" that are the basis of social studies teacher licensure (NCSS, 2000).

A disjuncture between what and how teachers study and what and how they are expected to teach doesn't appear to have changed substantially since critics were remarking on it during the New Social Studies movement of the 1960s. Back then, many teachers had simply never been prepared to think like a social scientist about the structure of disciplines, let alone model this to young people (Kownslar, 1974a). Small wonder the kind of playing with ideas predicted for the nation's classrooms never came to pass in most places. The recommendation or adoption in more recent years of social studies innovations such as document-based questions in assessments and internet-based project learning raises concerns about teacher education reminiscent of the 1960s:

> The teacher's academic background does not provide him with teaching models or curriculum organization consistent with basic characteristics of current social studies developments, i.e., teaching via inquiry, designing courses which are problem-centered or interdisciplinary, or teaching the structure of the disciplines. (Smith & Cox, 1969, pp. 158–159)

What kind of alternatives, assuming that there is no wholesale reorganization of the university, might we reasonably pursue?

One straightforward alternative already touched upon is encouragement of social science departments providing courses that treat the topics taught in the school curriculum much as what once happened in teachers' colleges. In other nations, this form of teacher education is the norm: Instead of taking the same courses as subject majors, teachers are prepared for a fundamental understanding of the concepts, principles, and procedures of school subjects (Ma, 1999). In the United States, this could take the form of pedagogically focused discussion sections attached to standard lecture courses such as "U.S. History Since 1877." Or, as in other nations, separate tracks could be created for teachers. Of course, this raises the problem of status. The predictable complaint is that such courses will be "watered down." In order to demonstrate that prospective teachers are as bright as any college students we often back down when this charge is leveled rather than presenting viable prototypes of such courses. As Whitehead (1929) noted, professional courses can, and should, be every bit as intellectual as academic courses "by promoting the imaginative consideration of the various general principles underlying that career" (p. 144).

In some years of working with able pre- and in-service teachers at the master's level—students who have a majored in a social science, most frequently history, at the nation's finest colleges and universities—I have found that few of these students ever seem to have considered how the two most prominent social studies, history and geography, are intertwined in how we make sense of the world. It is not, of course, that they are unable to grasp this connection once it is pointed out to them. Nevertheless, it is revealing that they apparently have never thought about it nor recall hearing it mentioned in their 4 years of undergraduate coursework. Thus, it should scarcely be surprising that these prospective educators equate the geographical dimension of history instruction, for example, with no more than pointing to the location of Gettysburg on a map rather than pondering: Why did Lee invade the North? Where might he have been headed and why there? What force was defending Richmond while Lee's army was in Pennsylvania? Why did Lincoln so passionately lament General Meade's failure to pursue the retreating Confederate army?

The relationship of physical phenomena (geography) and

social phenomena (history) in the lives of humans would be an ideal theme for a course to prepare teachers for instruction about the study of the United States. Regarding American history, especially the period of colonization, Dewey (1990) wrote:

> Since the aim is not "covering the ground," but knowledge of social processes used to secure social results, no attempt is made to go over the entire history, in chronological order, of America. Rather a series of types is taken up: Chicago and the northwestern Mississippi valley; Virginia, New York, and the Puritans and the Pilgrims in New England. The aim is to present a variety of climatic and local conditions, to show the different sorts of obstacles and helps that people found, and a variety of historic traditions and customs and purposes of different people. (p. 108)

The spirit of Dewey's view needs to extend to other courses in the social sciences as well: Why is population density normally greater around rivers and other bodies of water than other places? What has this to do with the emergence of the first civilizations in the river valleys of China, India, Mesopotamia, and Egypt? Can we see a related distribution of population in, say, contemporary Africa? How might this perspective help explain why early 19th-century Americans perceived the semi-arid Great Plains as the "Great American Desert"? How should powerful geographical generalizations be taught without their descending into the fallacy of geographic determinism, the belief that physical conditions dictate how human beings live?

Finally, in this section on subject matter preparation, one way to prepare liberal arts majors as teachers that has repeatedly recommended itself to policy- and opinion-makers is a special 5th-year program: Master of Arts in Teaching (MAT). The MAT degree was designed to "include work of varying amounts in the major academic field together with a moderate number of more-or-less orthodox courses in Education (often plus a professional seminar or two)" (Koerner, 1963, p. 170). A survey of the internet reveals that MAT programs are common in the United States today.

The MAT was invented, in large part, to attract able liberal arts graduates to teaching. It was assumed that this population held greater promise for teaching than persons who had devoted significant parts of their undergraduate work to education courses. The academic tenor of the MAT was intended to enhance its professional status relative to other teacher-preparation degrees, and seems to have done so.

At first glance, an overarching aim of the MAT idea is exciting: to stimulate the educational imaginations of the best and the brightest liberal arts graduates. Often, MAT programs involved the active collaboration of liberal arts and education faculty (Koerner, 1963, pp. 170–171), thus bridging the customary gulf between the two groups. Some anecdotal accounts suggest that the MAT succeeded in this aim for particular individuals, but how common this success has been is hard to say. Moreover, despite the endorsement of the MAT by academics and observers otherwise critical of teacher education programs, it does not appear to have been the subject of sustained analysis as an educational concept or to have been evaluated thoroughly except for there being a tallying of which institutions granted the MAT degree and the program components therein (see Elisberg, 1981).

It is unfortunate that we do not have better evidence on instruction in, and the effects of, the MAT, because enhanced academic preparation as a panacea for the ills of teacher education is such a recurring and apparently uncritically accepted notion. Naturally, the idea of greater depth in subject matter preparation appeals to social science academicians, but we do not have compelling evidence either of how much additional subject matter (or what kind) makes better teachers or if the MAT produces teachers who will be more likely to continue seeking professional growth (Elisberg, 1981, pp. 129–130).

Moreover, it is questionable (dead wrong, I think) if the relationship of subject matter and method is a simple linear one where subject matter knowledge comes first and then it is arranged for instructional purposes. Could the arrangement of, say, historical knowledge for instruction become for proficient educators a way of conceiving what historical knowledge is, what Erling Hunt (1935) once called "school history" rather than "scholar's history"? Is "school history," as historians seem to assume without much reflection, necessarily less significant knowledge than the contemporary interests of historians? During his lengthy involvement in the High School Geography Project of the 1960s, for instance, the geographer Robert McNee (1970) grew steadily more wary of assuming that academic expertise is the keystone of pedagogical improvement. After 5 years of attempting to disseminate new ideas and materials in geographic education, McNee expressed misgivings about the "one-directional movement of ideas which is assumed in the [diffusion] model." He observed that the geographer—whom he called the "thinker"—or the teacher trainer does not live in isolation.

> He is affected by the reception granted his ideas. Similarly, the teacher trainers do more than simply transmit or diffuse the ideas of the thinker. They affect the thinker by the feedback they give to him and they in turn are affected by the feedback from their pupils. And so on. (p. 88)

McNee's point is well taken. The transformation of scholarly content into subject matter suitable for school instruction is, for better or worse, not a one-way street. Neither competence in subject matter nor competence in method is alone sufficient to assure effective instruction (Hertzberg, 1988). Content enthusiasts routinely and wrongly cast method as "merely a species of classroom gimmickry or a set of tips for teaching," however, as if method were somehow antithetical to content (p. 38).

Although we may bemoan it, method is often treated as a string of expedients rather than an overall crafting of subject matter. At least judging from methods textbooks, relatively disembodied skills and emphases to be "infused" in the curriculum are singled out in methods courses. Map skills and gender equity are two cases in point. But rather than treat these skills and emphases in relative isolation, methods courses could embed them in the standard topics of the curriculum. For example, a fascinating application of map skills would be to trace the history of changing national boundaries of 20th-century Europe and their relationships to the two world wars, ethnic cleansing, and the Cold War (see Thornton, 2001b, in press). Similarly, rather than admonitions to teach for gender awareness supported by no more than illustrative snippets, it may be more effective for teacher education to examine in some depth how treatment of standard topics such as the antebellum period of U.S. history becomes altered by applying the lens of gender (see, for example, Crocco, 1997; Levstik, 2002). This suggests, as I take up in the following section, that method preparation should be weighted toward the standard topics of the curriculum rather than expedients and exceptional issues.

OBSTACLES TO EFFECTIVE METHODS COURSES

Although the subject-specific or special-methods course in social studies has traditionally been regarded as a cornerstone of teacher education programs, it has still been much maligned (see Patrick, 1973; Robinson, 1982). Expectations for the course are high—probably unrealistically so—and outcomes frequently disappoint teachers and observers. With some regularity, critics suggest that methods could be effectively taught in settings other than the methods course, such as on the job (e. g., Paige, 2002). Even the critics, however, seem to allow that generally it is more efficient for teachers to be prepared in methods rather than their learning entirely through trial and error. The limited body of research, moreover, supports the intuitive belief that focused, subject-specific methods courses contribute to effective teaching (Cruickshank & Associates, 1996; Education Commission of the States, 2003). Somewhere, as the historian and sometime curriculum developer Edwin Fenton (1967) pointed out, "someone must tie up the loose ends" in teacher education programs (p. 112).

It is not my intention to add to the already ample critiques of methods instruction; good summaries of them are available (e.g., Whitson, 2004). Rather, I will dwell on the course's potential. It is the single course that most social studies teachers are likely to have in common. Fenton (1967) judged it "potentially the single most important course which a future teacher can take" (p. 112).

The fact that so many prospective teachers hold high expectations for the methods course is a clue to its potential. From this perspective, their criticisms of what a methods course effectively did or did not do seems more of a reflection of their disappointment in the course rather than the *idea* of the course. Disappointment, after all, stems from hopeful expectations. It is hard to imagine significant numbers of novice teachers lacking interest in methods, the course they ordinarily consider the most "practical" on-campus education work they do.

As Fenton (1967) suggests, the methods course potentially deals with questions and materials vital to informed and purposeful teaching:

It can raise all the questions which other courses may have missed or have explored in isolation: What are the objectives of social studies education in the schools? Are they the same goals as for college social science course? What are sensible criteria for the selection of content? What methods of teaching do objectives imply? What materials are available? How should we group students for instruction? The methods teacher can assemble materials from the social studies projects to show his students. He can make himself a model of good instructional practices by teaching sample lessons to his class, as if he were a high school teacher and they a group of tenth graders. (p. 112)

Since this already daunting list compiled in the 1960s still more topics have (legitimately) demanded greater attention or been added to customary expectations for the methods course. Thus, in a course that students already approach with high expectations, the infusion of still more targeted emphases is now demanded. Targeted concerns for methods courses may now include, to mention just a few examples, aforementioned sensitivity to gender issues, cultural pluralism, genocide, free enterprise, economics, patriotism, financial education, and environmental awareness (Thornton, 2001a, p. 75). To be sure, such concerns are not *only* the responsibility of the methods course, but, because the course tries to "tie up the loose ends," there are great expectations that targeted concerns will appear somewhere in the course (e.g., Banks, 2001, p. 14; Segall, 2002, pp. 116–120). Not to treat them may be interpreted as being out of step with the times (Crocco, 2003–2004), even insensitive.

By now it should be clear that even the most imaginative methods course faces almost insurmountable demands on its time and design. Sometimes a second methods course is added; this may mitigate the problem but fails to solve it: "One or two courses out of the 40 or more which the typical undergraduate takes," Fenton (1967) sensibly noted, "cannot be expected to revolutionize his attitudes to teaching or to provide him with a full kit of useful tools" (p. 110). This reasoning leads us back to a key point in the preceding section: the necessity for greater coordination of social science courses with the methods course.

Perhaps the most significant thing the methods course by itself can contribute to teacher development is imbuing a sense of purpose and resultant efficacy. As Keith Barton and Linda Levstik (2004) tellingly concluded after a thorough review of studies of history teaching and teacher education:

Unless they [teachers] have a clear sense of purpose, teachers' primary actions continue to be coverage of the curriculum and control of students no matter how much they know about history, teaching, or the intersection of the two. (p. 258)

Most new teachers, and perhaps experienced teachers too, seem to yearn for a purposeful basis for method (see Cruickshank & Associates, 1996, p. 24; Kauffman et al., 2002). In the final analysis, however, educating for purposeful teaching must be connected to working with actual subject matter and, whether through simulated or actual experience, with some particular group of students. Given limited time, what types of learning activities are most likely to provide novice teachers with purpose and the wherewithal to let it guide instruction?

TOWARD MORE EFFECTIVE METHODS

From the outset, it should be made clear in the methods course that method is more than content-neutral instructional technique or strategy. Method includes both the nature of the particular subject matter and the purposes held for it. Although a clear distinction between what to teach and how to teach may be useful for purposes of discussion, the distinction breaks down in practice. Dewey (1966) was emphatic about this: "Method is not antithetical to subject matter; it is the effective direction of subject matter to desired results. It is antithetical to random and ill-considered action—ill-considered signifying ill-adapted" (p. 165).

It is precisely method as "ill-considered action" that has dogged social studies instruction from Dewey's day till the present. For example, Dewey wrote of how it manifested itself in geography as

a veritable rag-bag of intellectual odds and ends: the height of a mountain here, the course of a river there, the quantity of shingles produced in this town, the tonnage of shipping in that, the boundary of a country, the capital of a state. (p. 211)

Or, at the other end of the 20th century, Noddings (1998b) recalled:

Recently, one of my students—a pre-service graduate student in teacher education—described the world history course she was

assigned to teach. What an abominable hodge-podge it was: bits on
the fall of Rome, the Islamic empire, ancient China, feudal Japan,
ancient Africa (Ghana, Mali, Songhai only), European feudalism, the
Renaissance, and ancient Americas. (pp. 6–7)

It follows that a first tenet of method to be instilled is the
salience of subject matter selectivity. This is not to say that there
is one way or a sole criterion for selecting subject matter. Rather,
some defensible principle must guide subject matter selection.
Harold Rugg (1939), for example, noted that "one could not
'know' all the peoples of the earth" in the time available in the
school curriculum. His "principle of selection" was "the loyalties,
attitudes, problems, concepts and meanings indispensable to the
cultivated and intelligent man" and "those multitudinous examples of social life needed for illustrative clarification, any sample
of which would serve as effectively as another" (p. 153).
Significantly, Rugg, unlike learning-standards makers since the
1990s, was vigilant about what is truly indispensable, thus modeling an important element of method for teachers.

It should be possible in a methods course to spend a class or
two on each of the courses the teacher will be expected to teach.
This would allow for treating methods in context rather than as
discrete entities. For high school teachers, for example, this would
certainly include U.S. history and government, some global geography and history, and probably economics and current events as
well. For each school course, the methods course could treat what
material is intrinsically important, what is important for other
topics, what is enrichment material, recommended curriculum
materials, and so on.

But it would also be important in this walk through the curriculum to have a guided investigation of a sample topic or two of
unit length and consider some illustrative methods. For example,
for a global history course, World War I is a major topic for its own
sake but also for its many connections to other topics in the
course, such as nationalism, ethnic cleansing, internationalism,
and warfare in the industrial age. The methods instructor might
validate teacher presentations as a method for complex cause-
effect sequences such as the European diplomatic crisis of the
summer of 1914. Students might critique a video from a pedagogical perspective. For example, *The Smell of War* (Granada
Productions, 1988) well demonstrates how Europeans in 1914,
especially in the United Kingdom, were largely absorbed in the

affairs of daily life and the assassination of an unknown prince in a far-off Balkan land seemed only remotely connected to their lives. Did Europeans really welcome war, as has so often been asserted? The instructor might further question the common curricular practice of sharply dividing the war's "causes" from its conduct by noting that the aims of the Great Powers were in flux, and many causes, consequently, had little to do with articulated pre-war aims. Current events connections could be drawn to present and recent ethnic turbulence in the Balkans. Map skills could be illustrated showing the vital significance of the (English) Channel ports for the German military campaign in "neutral" Belgium and France. The war poets, among them Siegfried Sassoon, Wilfred Owen, and Robert Graves, could be examined as primary sources of the disenchantment, disorientation, and bewilderment that the war brought to Europeans who had once led settled lives. In this and other units, the instructor could also speak to individualization of instruction through, for instance, enrichment work.

This approach of walking teachers through the curriculum offers several advantages. For example, first it refreshes students' knowledge of the subject matter and perhaps recasts and broadens it as well. Second, it demonstrates that the arrangement of material for instruction is not always identical with how scholars might arrange it. Third, it models how history instruction can be enriched through work in map skills, in literature, and in the use of media other than the printed word and by drawing comparisons with today's world.

Consideration of representative units also suggests the concern of the following section: extended scrutiny of curriculum materials in methods courses. Although curriculum materials, especially textbooks, are ubiquitous in social studies classrooms—indeed, their alleged overuse is a frequent target of criticism—their teacher education potential has received scant systematic attention (see Ball & Cohen, 1996).

METHOD AND CURRICULUM MATERIALS

All teachers are either creators or consumers (or both) of curriculum materials. In any case, they must, in some way, appraise materials, because the very act of selection of materials is an evaluative act. As with curricular-instructional gatekeeping in general, however, the fact that teachers must employ some criterion to select materials does not necessarily imply that their criteria are well-founded or conscious. Unless materials are expected to teach themselves, teachers must bring purpose to the selection and use of materials.

Appraisal of curriculum materials is an authentic task in teacher education because it presents simultaneous academic and professional demands. Of course, the academic element of this process has apparent use for teacher reflection on curricular content, an advantage upon which methods instructors do not seem to capitalize very often. It is also significant that examination of curriculum materials may give some prospective teachers their first opportunity to encounter material deliberately arranged for instruction and learning; such opportunities can easily have been absent in their undergraduate educations (Wilson & McDiarmid, 1996). Perhaps in geography materials they could compare, for instance, how the location of manufacturing industry was treated in the discovery materials of the 1960s, in computer simulations today, and through current textbooks.

Recognizing the dual academic and professional advantages of working with curriculum materials, curriculum developers have sometimes involved teachers in creating curriculum. Elliot Eisner (1975), for example, has worked with teachers once curriculum specialists have designed a basic curriculum structure and prototype materials. Although requiring close consultation with developers or other authorities, teachers can profitably create their own materials (pp. 166–167). This approach contributes to the growth of teachers in a way that is "practical and concrete"; "at the same time it requires teachers to consider concepts such as continuity and sequence as well as other matters that so often appear to teachers to be little more than educational slogans" (p. 167).

Even with ready-made materials, however, methods instructors themselves may not know about or use the latest innovations (Switzer, 1993). Technological advances make this issue more urgent. The proliferation of websites on the internet is a particularly important case in point. It is vital that teachers are prepared for evaluating websites. Specifically, they need to learn educational criteria for appraising the worth—especially the reliability—of websites, including at a metalevel of evaluating websites that present evaluations of websites. This kind of metaevaluation might entail, say, developing rubrics to evaluate rubric websites. All this should help teachers reinforce a healthy skepticism that reliable knowledge can ever be easily found.

Teachers may also benefit from experience in curriculum planning rather than just consuming someone else's curriculum plans. Often teachers do become involved in local curriculum-development initiatives. Even more frequently, they may engage in disseminating new curriculum materials to peers, mentoring student teachers in the arrangement of subject matter, and being involved in related curricular dimensions of teaching. For example, in many places they are expected to help design interdisciplinary curriculum (Crocco & Thornton, 2002) or implement block scheduling (Flinders, 2000). But teachers are seldom adequately trained in curriculum construction—their formal experience may have been no more than lesson and unit planning in a methods course. Unless teachers are educated in curriculum work they will likely lack the ability to harness those materials and learning opportunities to the most desirable educational uses. Teacher education, in other words, requires a "curricular base" (Zumwalt, 1989).

CONCLUSION

It is important to note that this discussion of the methods course is far from complete. Major elements of classroom teacher-student teacher encounters are absent. For example, almost everything discussed in this chapter should be tempered by the relational demands of teaching. How is the effectiveness of method enhanced by, say, continuity between the same teacher and same group of students (e.g., Flinders & Noddings, 2001)? Or we could look at the effects of the school reform movement on method (e.g., Thornton, 2004b). But my intention in this chapter has been to underscore the relationship between method and subject matter in teacher education. Leaving teachers to work out this relationship for themselves appears to undermine almost everything else in social studies curriculum change.

7

Enactment of Curriculum That Matters

The curriculum and teaching offered by a school are, whatever else, gatekeeping devices. So, too, is the program of study and teaching in teacher education. In both settings, students encounter some ideas and skills and do not encounter other ideas and skills. What we have an opportunity to learn and how we interact with it are powerful predictors of what we are likely to come to know and value. Curricular-instructional gatekeeping is a way of altering the intellect of students; it is also a way of influencing their morals. As Philip Jackson (1992) observed, "Teaching after all is a profession in which the practitioners, in the main, are bent on doing good" (p. 18). It is not as if educators have a choice whether they will tend the curricular-instructional gate—it is inevitable. As I have noted more than once above, inevitability does not imply the educational desirability of answers to the questions if, when, how much, for what reasons, and to whom the gate opens. Nor does it imply that the gate's manipulation by the teacher is even done with much conscious thought. But done it is. Thus educators' purposes, and how they act on them, matter.

Teacher gatekeeping takes place in a fluid and uncertain environment. Teachers interpret what a curriculum means and shape instruction to illuminate somehow those meanings for their students. Given the perplexing number of factors involved in gatekeeping—Jackson (1968) once suggested, for instance, that elementary teachers engage in as many as 1,000 interpersonal interchanges each day (p. 11)—it cannot be an "exact science." I believe that how Milbrey McLaughlin (1997) described the implementation of open education programs gets at the nature of how all gatekeeping works: "These practices are not based on a 'model' of classroom organization change to be strictly followed, but on a common set of convictions about the nature of learning and the purpose of teaching" (p. 167). Although all teachers plainly do not share a set of convictions, the convictions they *do* hold deeply influence their gatekeeping. These convictions may not be articulated or formalized enough to constitute a model coherent to a stranger, but they drive teachers' pedagogy.

Educators' convictions, as we have seen, can drive educational aims in a range of directions. Nel Noddings (2003a) writes, for instance, of social studies aims: "History, geography, and natural history offer the promise of self-understanding on the level of groups and whole societies, and self-understanding is crucial to both citizenship and personal happiness" (p. 254). But these aims are realized—perhaps at the level of curriculum development, perhaps in instructional planning and interactive teaching, probably some combination of both—by how the gate is tended.

Consider Switzerland as a topic. A good deal of significant subject matter in the Noddings sense above springs to mind: physical geography such as glaciation and its relationships to contemporary settlement patterns, the mountainous terrain and its relationships to transhumance or tourism. Traditional Swiss neutrality also suggests itself; perhaps links could be made to Hemingway's (1929) characters in *A Farewell to Arms* fleeing the Great War for the haven of Switzerland. Or consideration could be given to banking and its relationships to Swiss policies on immigration and trade with Nazi Germany as well as subsequent controversies about compensation and possible tacit Swiss acceptance of some Nazi policies. Or diversity, how different ethnic groups, often isolated by mountains (at least traditionally), as well as religious and linguistic diversity, nonetheless became the basis of a workable nation state. As a cross-cultural comparison, how might the example of diverse, mountainous Switzerland compare with diverse, mountainous Afghanistan?

In this Switzerland example we need goals in order to settle on what principles, concepts, and relationships to select for study. Many of the identified relationships seem significant, and possibly all of them will lead back to most of the same information. As gatekeepers, however, we would want to select which ideas and relationships and information to pursue based on our purposes, such as social competence, personal efficacy, civic participation, and shared cultural knowledge. The topic is rich in material that is relevant to each of these purposes.

We always need to ask why a topic should be studied. Relationships (and information) about Switzerland or many other topics too often appear in the curriculum for shallow reasons, say, in the cause of interdisciplinary curriculum, when the social studies contribution is treatment of a "mountain" country. A good deal of superficial work, with insufficient thought given to purposes, has been done under the label of interdisciplinary curriculum. Simply combining material from different academic subjects fails to guarantee that any significant educational objective will be addressed. Prior questions such as the following need to be asked: What topics do we want to study and how are they connected to our main aims and other topics? How well suited is interdisciplinary work for these topics? Does such work significantly enhance the meanings of the topics or does it simply create more complicated instructional planning? A rule of thumb may be that method should follow substance, which is primarily determined by purpose.

Despite the salience of purpose, much energy has been expended in social studies education over whether we should teach x or y. It is questionable how much these battles matter when the information is divorced from any pedagogical context. An example of the disputes was the caustic debate in the 1990s over matters such as whether Harriet Tubman is more important to know about than Thomas Edison. Or, as I noticed recently when thumbing through a world history textbook, Vietnam was included but not the Philippines. Should that disturb us? In fact, it is difficult to make a cogent case for why anyone would need to know much of what we require young people to study. Why must every young American know why ancient kingdoms in Indo-China rose and fell or what were the major battles of the Civil War? Note that I am not arguing that this material is trivial—that young people should not study it—but I am saying that a stronger case than is usually made is necessary. Much of what we teach in social studies does not directly help us in day-to-day life, but that outcome is often as much a product of how the material is approached as anything intrinsic to it.

What won't do much good is to simply insist that all young Americans learn certain material. It may effectively coerce learning, but it is unlikely to persuade most students that the material matters. The information transmitted today is forgotten a few days later. But attempts to specify what truly is basic usually bog down in a variety of predictable battles. One battle is to please what each of the constituent social science groups thinks is necessary, and this has tended to end up in a process of comparing apples and oranges in terms of what is meant by a concept or the structure of the discipline, and so on (see Goetz, 1994; Price, Hickman, & Smith, 1965). Some of these ideas that were very useful pedagogically were discarded possibly because academicians and others insisted on construing them rigidly (Parsons & Shaftel, 1967). Other pressures come from the insistence of numerous groups that their group or cause be included in the curriculum—the result is "mentioning" in a superficial narrative that shortchanges everyone. We hear tales, for example, or see photographs, of people whose inclusion in the text is not really explained.

But it should be possible to achieve wider, probably not universal, agreement on what concepts, skills, and principles are truly things everyone should know. The rest could then properly be left to local discretion. For instance, we would probably agree that all Americans should know something about the ways of life of the continent's aboriginal peoples. Although all would explore principles of human-environmental relationships, the particular information may be better chosen locally. So in an Arizona school different Native Americans from a Pennsylvania school might be selected for study, even though much of the conceptual learning would be comparable.

Instructional arrangements would also benefit from a loosening of conventions. The teacher should act more as a guide—opening gates students want to go through, that is—than a director. As explored in earlier chapters, for instance, there is latitude in many places to give students choice in what they study. Even for required material, some teachers have employed learning stations to capitalize as far as they can on student learning modalities and interests. Moreover, it should be emphasized that employing alternative models of instruction is not an all-or-nothing proposition. As noted, even occasional instruction that lights a spark can do much to enliven the classroom curriculum in other areas.

It seems to follow that most of what I am recommending is unlikely to happen unless we reconsider teacher education. It is scarcely surprising that teachers who have never conceived of themselves as guides rather than directors of what their students study or have themselves experienced project learning might balk at such departures from instructional norms. So teachers need to encounter not only subject matters more relevant to the demands of the school curriculum in their preparation. They also need to experience subject matter in quite different ways (see Griffin, 1942; Rodgers, 2001; Rogers, 1969). We must also underscore— better yet, have them learn firsthand—that such an approach is harder to do than the well-trodden "learn the traditional academic subjects and water them down for kids."

Finally, we need far more examples, well-documented ones, of enacting social studies curricula, including of how such curricula were developed or modified at the local level. These examples are not necessarily for replication, although there is nothing wrong with thoughtful adaptation, but to show what is possible, how it might be done, what the trade-offs are, and so forth. In other words, we could truly do educational development and build on what others have learned rather than returning to the start with each new cure-all that comes down the pike. Perhaps then we can give tangible meaning to Dewey's (1966) aspiration for our students in social studies: "Thus our ordinary daily experiences cease to be things of the moment and gain enduring substance" (p. 209). Educators then truly would be teaching social studies that matters.

References

Adler, M. J. (1982). *The Paideia proposal.* New York: Macmillan.

Alleman, J., & Brophy, J. (1993a). Is curriculum integration a boon or a threat to social studies? *Social Education, 57,* 287–291.

Alleman, J., & Brophy, J. (1993b). Teaching that lasts: College students' reports of learning activities experienced in elementary school social studies. *Social Science Record, 30*(2), 36–48.

American Historical Association. (1899). *The study of history in schools.* New York: Macmillan.

Armento, B. J. (1996). The professional development of social studies teachers. In J. Sikula, T. J. Buttery, & E. Guyton (Eds.), *Handbook of research on teacher education* (2nd ed., pp. 485–502). New York: Macmillan.

Bain, R. B. (2000). Into the breach: Using research and theory to shape history instruction. In P. N. Stearns, P. Seixas, & S. Wineburg (Eds.), *Knowing, teaching, and learning history* (pp. 331–352). New York: New York University Press.

Ball, D. L., & Cohen, D. K. (1996). Reform by the book: What is—or might be—the role of curriculum materials in teacher learning and instructional reform? *Educational Researcher, 25*(9), 6–8, 14.

Banks, J. A. (2001). Citizenship education and diversity: Implications for teacher education. *Journal of Teacher Education, 52*(1), 5–16.

Barton, K. C., & Levstik, L. S. (2004). *Teaching history for the common good.* Mahwah, NJ: Erlbaum.

Beard, C. A. (1932). *A charter for the social sciences in the schools.* New York: Scribner's.

Bennett, W. J. (1987). *James Madison High School: A curriculum for American students.* Washington, DC: U.S. Department of Education.

Ben-Peretz, M. (1975). The concept of curriculum potential. *Curriculum Theory Network, 5,* 151–159.

Berger, E., & Winters, B. A. (1973). *Social studies in the open classroom.* New York: Teachers College Press.

Bestor, A. (1953). *Educational wastelands: The retreat from learning in our public schools.* Urbana: University of Illinois Press.

Beyer, B. K. (1994). Gone but not forgotten: Reflections on the New Social Studies. *The Social Studies, 85,* 251–256.

Bowman, I. (1934). *Geography in relation to the social sciences.* New York: Scribner's.

Bradley Commission on History in Schools. (1988). *Building a history curriculum: Guidelines for teaching history in schools.* Washington, DC: Educational Excellence Network.

Brickhouse, N. (2003). Telephone interview, August 18.

Brophy, J. (Ed.). (2001). *Subject-specific instructional methods and activities.* Oxford: Elsevier Science.

Brophy, J., & Alleman, J. (2000). Primary grade students' knowledge and thinking about Native American and pioneer homes. *Theory and Research in Social Education, 28,* 96–120.

Brophy, J., Prawat, R., & McMahon, S. (1991). Social education professors and elementary teachers: Two purviews on elementary social studies. *Theory and Research in Social Education, 19,* 173–188.

Bruner, J. S. (1960). *The process of education.* Cambridge: Harvard University Press.

Cassidy, E. W., & Kurfman, D. G. (1977). Decision making as purpose and process. In D. G. Kurfman (Ed.), *Developing decision-making skills* (pp. 1–26). Arlington, VA: National Council for the Social Studies.

Connelly, F. M., & Ben-Peretz, M. (1997). Teachers, research, and curriculum development. In D. J. Flinders & S. J. Thornton (Eds.), *The curriculum studies reader* (pp. 178–187). New York: Routledge.

Cornett, J. W. (1990). Teacher thinking about curriculum and instruction: A case study of a secondary social studies teacher. *Theory and Research in Social Education, 18,* 248–273.

Cremin, L. A. (1990). *Popular education and its discontents.* New York: Harper & Row.

Crocco, M. S. (1997). Making time for women's history...when your survey course is already filled to overflowing. *Social Education, 61,* 32–37.

Crocco, M. S. (2003–2004). Dealing with difference in the social studies: A historical perspective. *International Journal of Social Education, 18*(2), 106–126.

Crocco, M. S., & Thornton, S. J. (2002). Social studies in the New York City public schools: A descriptive study. *Journal of Curriculum and Supervision, 17,* 206–231.

Cronbach, L. J. (1966). The logic of experiments on discovery. In L. S. Shulman & E. R. Keislar (Eds.), *Learning by discovery* (pp. 76–92). Chicago: Rand McNally.

Cruickshank, D. R., & Associates. (1996). *Preparing America's teachers.* Bloomington, IN: Phi Delta Kappa.

Cuban, L. (1991). History of teaching in social studies. In J. P. Shaver (Ed.), *Handbook of research on social studies teaching and learning* (pp. 197–209). New York: Macmillan.

Cuban, L. (1999). *How scholars trumped teachers: Change without reform in university curriculum, teaching, and research, 1890–1990.* New York: Teachers College Press.

Curti, M. (1959). *The social ideas of American educators* (Rev. ed.).

Totowa, NJ: Littlefield, Adams.

Darling-Hammond, L. (1999). Educating teachers for the next century: Rethinking practice and policy. In G. Griffin (Ed.), *The education of teachers* (pp. 221–256). Chicago: National Society for the Study of Education.

Dewey, J. (1963). *Experience and education.* New York: Collier.

Dewey, J. (1966). *Democracy and education.* New York: Free Press.

Dewey, J. (1969). What is social study? In R. E. Gross, W. E. McPhie, & J. R. Fraenkel (Eds.), *Teaching the social studies: What, why, and how* (pp. 5–7). Scranton, PA: International Textbook Company.

Dewey, J. (1975). *Interest and effort in education.* Carbondale: Southern Illinois University Press.

Dewey, J. (1990). *The school and society; and, The child and the curriculum.* Chicago: University of Chicago Press.

Dewey, J. (1991a). The challenge of democracy to education. In J. A. Boydston (Ed.), *The later works, 1925–1953* (Vol. 11, pp. 181–190). Carbondale: Southern Illinois University Press.

Dewey, J. (1991b). What is learning? In J. A. Boydston (Ed.), *The later works, 1925–1953 (Vol. 11)* (pp. 238–242). Carbondale: Southern Illinois University Press.

Dewey, J. (1997). My pedagogic creed. In D. J. Flinders & S. J. Thornton (Eds.), *The curriculum studies reader* (pp. 17–23). New York: Routledge.

Education Commission of the States. (2003). *Eight questions on teacher preparation: What does the research say?* Denver: Author.

Egan, K. (1999). *Children's minds, talking rabbits, and clockwork oranges.* New York: Teachers College Press.

Eisner, E. W. (1975). Curriculum development in Stanford's Kettering Project: Recollections and ruminations. In J. Schaffarzick & D. H. Hampson (Eds.), *Strategies for curriculum development* (pp. 147–168). Berkeley, CA: McCutchan.

Eisner, E. W. (1982). *Cognition and curriculum: A basis for deciding what to teach.* New York: Longman.

Eisner, E. W. (1985). *What high schools are like: Views from the inside* (Stanford-in-the-Schools-Project: Curriculum Panel Report). Stanford, CA: Stanford University.

Eisner, E. W. (2002). *The educational imagination: On the design and evaluation of school programs* (3rd ed.). Upper Saddle River, NJ: Merrill Prentice Hall.

Elisberg, J. S. (1981). *A study of selected Master of Arts in Teaching programs in the United States.* Unpublished doctoral dissertation, Northwestern University, Evanston, IL.

Elson, R. M. (1964). *Guardians of tradition: American schoolbooks of the nineteenth century.* Lincoln: University of Nebraska Press.

Engle, S. H., & Longstreet, W. S. (1972). *A design for social education in the open curriculum.* New York: Harper & Row.

Engle, S. H., & Ochoa, A. S. (1988). *Education for democratic citizenship: Decision making in the social studies.* New York: Teachers College Press.

Epstein, T. L. (2001). Racial identity and young peoples' perspectives on social education. *Theory into Practice, 40,* 42–47.

Evans, R.W. (2004). *The social studies wars.* New York: Teachers College Press.

Fenton, E. (1967). *The new social studies.* New York: Holt, Rinehart & Winston.

Fine, M. (1995). *Habits of mind: Struggling over values in America's classrooms.* San Francisco: Jossey-Bass.

Flinders, D. J. (1996). Teaching for cultural literacy: A curriculum study. *Journal of Curriculum and Supervision, 11,* 351–366.

Flinders, D. J. (Ed.). (2000). *Block scheduling: Restructuring the school day.* Bloomington, IN: Phi Delta Kappa.

Flinders, D. J., & Noddings, N. (2001). *Multiyear teaching: The case for continuity.* Bloomington, IN: Phi Delta Kappa.

Geography Education Standards Project. (1994). *Geography for life: National geography standards.* Washington, DC: National Geographic Research & Exploration.

Global Security. (2004). *Vozrozhdeniye Island Renaissance/ Rebirth Island.* Author. Retrieved January 29, from the World Wide Web: http://www.globalsecurity.org/wmd/world/russia/vozrozhdenly.htm

Goetz, W. W. (1994). The new social studies: The memoir of a practitioner. *The Social Studies, 85,* 100–105.

Goodlad, J. I. (1966). *The changing school curriculum.* New York: Fund for the Advancement of the Humanities.

Goodlad, J. I. (1984). *A place called school.* New York: McGraw-Hill.

Goodlad, J. I. (1994). *What schools are for* (2nd ed.). Bloomington, IN: Phi Delta Kappa.

Granada Productions (1988). *The smell of war.* Princeton, NJ: Films for the Humanities.

Grant, S. G. (2003). *History lessons: Teaching, learning, and testing in U.S. high school classrooms.* Mahwah, NJ: Erlbaum.

Griffin, A.F. (1942). *A philosophical approach to the subject-matter preparation of teachers of history.* Unpublished doctoral dissertation, Ohio State University, Columbus.

Griffin, G. A. (1999). Changes in teacher education: Looking to the future. In G. A. Griffin (Ed.), *The education of teachers* (pp. 1–28). Chicago: National Society for the Study of Education.

Gross, R. E. (1958). United States history. In R. E. Gross & L. D. Zeleny (Eds.), *Educating citizens for democracy* (pp. 162–214). New York: Oxford University Press.

Gruenwald, D. A. (2003). Foundations of place: A multi-disciplinary framework for place-conscious education. *American Educational Research Journal, 40,* 619–654.

Haggerty, M. E. (1935). The low visibility of educational issues. *School and Society, 41,* 273–283.

Hamilton, D. (1975). Handling innovation in the classroom: Two Scottish examples. In W. A. Reid & D. F. Walker (Eds.), *Case studies in curriculum change: Great Britain and the United States* (pp. 179–207). London: Routledge & Kegan Paul.

Harper, C. A. (1938). This matter of method. *Social Education, 2,* 392–394.

Hawkins, D. (1973). How to plan for spontaneity. In C. E. Silberman (Ed.), *The open classroom reader* (pp. 486–503). New York: Vintage.

Hemingway, E. (1929). *A farewell to arms.* New York: Scribner's.

Herbst, HJ. (1989). *And sadly teach: Teacher education and professionalization in American culture.* Madison, WI: University of Wisconsin Press.

Hertzberg, H. W. (1981). *Social studies reform, 1880–1980.* Boulder, CO: Social Science Education Consortium.

Hertzberg, H. W. (1988). Are method and content enemies? In B. R. Gifford (Ed.), *History in the schools* (pp. 13–40). New York: Macmillan.

Hess, D. E. (2002). Discussing controversial public issues in secondary social studies classrooms: Learning from skilled teachers. *Theory and Research in Social Education, 30,* 10–41.

Hiebert, J., Gallimore, R., & Stigler, J. W. (2002). A knowledge base for the teaching profession: What would it look like and how can we get one? *Educational Researcher, 31*(5), 3–15.

Hirsch, E. D., Jr. (1987). *Cultural literacy: What every American needs to know.* Boston: Houghton Mifflin.

Hoffenbacher, H. B. (1958). American society and social problems. In R. E. Gross & L. D. Zeleny (Eds.), *Educating citizens for democracy* (pp. 215–246). New York: Oxford University Press.

Hunt, E. M. (1935). Scholars' history versus school history. *The Social Studies, 26,* 513–517.

Hunt, E. M. (1944). Editor's page. *Social Education, 8,* 53–56.

Illinois Curriculum Program. (1971). Students develop the concept of "imperialism." In B. K. Beyer & A. N. Penna (Eds.), *Concepts in the social studies* (pp. 67–75). Washington, DC: National Council for the Social Studies.

Jackson, P. W. (1968). *Life in classrooms.* New York: Holt, Rinehart & Winston.

Jackson, P. W. (1992). *Untaught lessons.* New York: Teachers College Press.

Jenness, D. (1990). *Making sense of social studies.* New York: Macmillan.

Kauffman, D., Johnson, S. M., Kardos, S. M., Liu, E., & Peske, H. G. (2002). "Lost at sea": New teachers' experiences with curriculum and assessment. *Teachers College Record, 104,* 273–300.

Kentworthy, L. (1970). *Guide to social studies teaching* (3rd ed.). Belmont, CA: Wadsworth.

Kliebard, H. M. (1979). Systematic curriculum development, 1890–1959. In J. Schaffarzick & G. Sykes (Eds.), *Value conflicts and curriculum issues* (pp. 197–236). Berkeley, CA: McCutchan.

Koerner, J. D. (1963). *The miseducation of American teachers.* Boston: Houghton Mifflin.

Kohn, A. (2004). Test today, privatize tomorrow: Using accountability to "reform" public schools to death. *Phi Delta Kappan, 85,* 569–577.

Kownslar, A. O. (1974a). Is history relevant? In A. O. Kownslar (Ed.), *Teaching American history: The quest for relevancy* (pp. 3–15). Washington, DC: National Council for the Social Studies.

Kownslar, A. O. (Ed.). (1974b). *Teaching American history: The quest for relevancy.* Washington, DC: National Council for the Social Studies.

Lagemann, E. C. (1992). Prophecy or profession? George S. Counts and the social study of education. *American Journal of Education, 100,* 137–165.

Levstik, L. S. (1996). NCSS and the teaching of history. In O. L. Davis, Jr. (Ed.), *NCSS in retrospect* (pp. 21–34). Washington, DC: National Council for the Social Studies.

Levstik, L. S. (2002). "Scary thing being an eighth grader": Exploring gender and sexuality in a middle school U.S. history unit. *Theory and Research in Social Education, 30,* 233–254.

Libresco, A., & Wolfe, J. (2003). Moving students from personal to global awareness. *Social Education, 67,* 44–46.

Longstreet, W. S. (1973). The school's curriculum. In J. I. Goodlad & H. G. Shane (Eds.), *The elementary school in the United States* (pp. 243–271). Chicago: National Society for the Study of Education.

Ma, L. (1999). *Knowing and teaching elementary mathematics: Teachers' understanding of fundamental mathematics in China and the United States.* Mahwah, NJ: Erlbaum.

MacDonald, J. B. (2003). *State curriculum policies and teachers' practice: The experiences of three New York State social studies teachers.* Unpublished doctoral dissertation, Columbia University, New York.

Madsen, J., Fifield, S., Allen, D., Shipman, H., Brickhouse, N., Ford, D., & Dagher, Z. (2001, December). *A science semester at the University of Delaware: Integrated inquiry- and problem-based approach to improve the science understanding of future elementary education teachers.* Paper presented at the American Geophysical Union, Boston.

Marsden, W. E. (1995). *Geography 11–16: Rekindling good practice.* London: David Fulton.

Marsden, W. E. (2000). Geography and two centuries of education for peace and international understanding. *Geography, 85,* 289–302.

Marsden, W. E. (2001). *The school textbook: Geography, history, and social studies.* London: Woburn Press.

Marshall, L. C., & Goetz, R. M. (1936). *Curriculum-making in the social studies: A social process approach.* New York: Scribner's.

McCutcheon, G. (1994). *Developing the curriculum: Solo and group deliberation.* White Plains, NY: Longman.

McCutcheon, G. (1997). Curriculum and the work of teachers. In D. J. Flinders & S. J. Thornton (Eds.), *The curriculum studies reader* (pp. 188–197). New York: Routledge.

McKee, S. J., & Day, A., L. (1992). The social studies methods course: A collaborative approach. *Social Education, 56,* 183–184.

McLaughlin, M. W. (1997). Implementation as mutual adaptation: Change in classroom organization. In D. J. Flinders & S. J. Thornton (Eds.), *The curriculum studies reader* (pp. 167–177). New York: Routledge.

McNee, R. B. (1970). The education of a geographer. In M. M. Krug, J. B. Poster, & W. B. Gillies, III (Eds.), *The new social studies: Analysis of theory and materials* (pp. 81–88). Itasca, IL: Peacock.

McNeil, L. M. (1986). *Contradictions of control: School structure and school knowledge.* New York: Routledge & Kegan Paul.

Mitchell, L. S. (1991). *Young geographers* (4th ed.). New York: Bank Street College of Education.

Moreau, J. (2003). *Schoolbook nation: Conflicts over American history textbooks from the Civil War to the present.* Ann Arbor: University of Michigan Press.

Muessig, R. H. (1987). An analysis of developments in geographic education. *Elementary School Journal, 87,* 519–530.

National Center for History in the Schools. (1995). *National standards for history* (Rev. ed.). Los Angeles: University of California at Los Angeles.

National Commission on Social Studies in the Schools. (1989). *Charting a course: Social studies for the 21st century.* Washington, DC: Author.

National Council for the Social Studies. (1994). *Expectations of excellence: Curriculum standards for social studies.* Washington, DC: Author.

National Council for the Social Studies. (2000). *Program standards for the initial preparation of social studies teachers.* Washington, DC: Author.

National Education Association. (1893). *Report of the Committee on History, Civil Government, and Political Economy.* Washington, DC: Government Printing Office.

National Education Association. (1994). The social studies in secondary education. In M. R. Nelson (Ed.), *The social studies in secondary education: A reprint of the seminal 1916 report with annotations and commentaries.* Bloomington, IN: ERIC Clearinghouse for Social Studies/Social Science Education.

Nelson, J. L. (2001). Defining social studies. In W. B. Stanley (Ed.), *Critical issues in social studies research for the 21st century* (pp. 15–38). Greenwich, CT: Information Age.

Nevins, A. (1942, June 21). American history for Americans. *The New York Times.*

Newmann, F. M. (1985). *Educational reform and social studies: Implications of six reports.* Boulder, CO: Social Science Education Consortium.

Noddings, N. (1979). NIE's national curriculum development conference. In J. Schaffarzick & G. Sykes (Eds.), *Value conflicts and curriculum issues* (pp. 291–312). Berkeley, CA: McCutchan.

Noddings, N. (1989). Theoretical and practical concerns about small groups in mathematics. *Elementary School Journal, 89,* 607–623.

Noddings, N. (1995). *Philosophy of education.* Boulder, CO: Westview Press.

Noddings, N. (1998a). Teachers and subject matter knowledge. *Teacher Education Quarterly, 25*(4), 86–89.

Noddings, N. (1998b, April). *Teaching for continuous learning.* Paper presented at the American Educational Research Association, San Diego.

Noddings, N. (2001). Care and coercion in school reform. *Journal of Educational Change, 2,* 35–43.

Noddings, N. (2002a). *Educating moral people.* New York: Teachers College Press.

Noddings, N. (2002b). *Starting at home: Caring and social policy.* Berkeley: University of California Press.

Noddings, N. (2003a). *Happiness and education.* Cambridge: Cambridge University Press.

Noddings, N. (2003b). Is teaching a practice? *Journal of Philosophy of Education, 37,* 241–251.

Novick, P. (1988). *The "objectivity question" and the American historical profession.* Cambridge: Cambridge University Press.

Ochoa, A. S. (1981). The education of social studies teachers. In H. D. Mehlinger & O. L. Davis, Jr. (Eds.), *The social studies* (pp. 151–169). Chicago: National Society for the Study of Education.

Ochoa-Becker, A. S. (2001). A critique of the NCSS curriculum standards. *Social Education, 65,* 165–168.

Oliver, D. W., & Shaver, J. P. (1966). *Teaching public issues in the high school.* Boston: Houghton Mifflin.

Orr, D. W. (2002). *The nature of design: Ecology, culture, and human intention.* Oxford: Oxford University Press.

Paige, R. (2001). *Remarks, Standards-Based Teacher Education (STEP) conference.* Retrieved August 13, 2003, from the World Wide Web: http://www.ed.gov/Speeches/06-2001/010612.html

Paige, R. (2002). *Meeting the highly qualified teachers challenge: The secretary's annual report on teacher quality.* Washington, DC: U.S. Department of Education.

Parker, W. C. (2003). *Teaching democracy: Unity and diversity in public life.* New York: Teachers College Press.

Parsons, T. W., & Shaftel, F. R. (1967). Thinking and inquiry: Some critical issues—instruction in the elementary grades. In J. Fair & F. R. Shaftel (Eds.), *Effective thinking in the social studies* (pp. 123–166). Washington, DC: National Council for the Social Studies.

Patrick, J. J. (1973). *Reforming the social studies methods course.* Boulder, CO: Social Science Education Consortium.

Pope, D. C. (2001). *"Doing school": How we are creating a generation of stressed out, materialistic, and miseducated students.* New Haven, CT: Yale University Press.

Price, R. A., Hickman, W., & Smith, G. (1965). *Major concepts for the social studies.* Syracuse, NY: Social Studies Curriculum Center, Syracuse University.

Pulsipher, L. M. (1999). *World regional geography.* New York: W. H. Freeman.

Ravitch, D. (1987). Tot sociology, or what happened to history in the grade schools. *American Scholar, 56,* 343–354.

Ravitch, D. (1989). The plight of history in American schools. In P. Gagnon & the Bradley Commission on History in Schools (Eds.), *Historical literacy: The case for history in American education* (pp. 51–68). New York: Macmillan.

Reeder, E. H. (1935). John Dewey and the activist movement. In E. B. Wesley (Ed.), *The historical approach to methods of teaching the social studies* (pp. 38–49). Philadelphia: McKinley.

Robinson, P. (1982, November). *Patterns in social studies methods courses: A review of the literature.* Paper presented at the National Council for the Social Studies, Boston.

Rodgers, C. R. (2001). "It's elementary": The central role of subject matter in learning, teaching, and learning to teach (Review of the book, *The roots of literacy*). *American Journal of Education, 109,* 472–480.

Rogers, C. (1969). *Freedom to learn.* Columbus, OH: Merrill.

Ross, E. W. (1997). The struggle for the social studies curriculum. In E. W. Ross (Ed.), *The social studies curriculum: Purposes, problems, and possibilities* (pp. 3–19). Albany: State University of New York Press.

Rothstein, R. (2004). We are not ready to assess history performance. *Journal of American History, 90,* 1381–1391.

Rugg, H. O. (1921). Reconstructing the curriculum. *Historical Outlook, 12,* 184–189.

Rugg, H. O. (1936). *American life and the school curriculum: Next steps toward schools of living.* Boston: Ginn.

Rugg, H. O. (1939). Curriculum-design in the social sciences: What I believe...In J. A. Michener (Ed.), *The future of the social studies: Proposals for an experimental social-studies curriculum* (pp. 140–158). Cambridge: National Council for the Social Studies.

Saxe, D. W. (1991). *Social studies in schools: A history of the early years.* Albany: State University of New York Press.

Schulten, S. (2001). *The geographical imagination in America, 1880–1950.* Chicago: University of Chicago Press.

Segall, A. (2002). *Disturbing practice: Reading teacher education as text.* New York: Peter Lang.

Shaver, J. P. (1977). A critical view of the social studies profession. *Social Education, 41,* 300–307.

Shaver, J. P. (1979). The usefulness of educational research in curricular/instructional decision-making in social studies. *Theory and Research in Social Education, 7*(3), 21–46.

Shaver, J. P. (1985). The social sciences and the civic education of teachers and administrators. In A. H. Jones (Ed.), *Civic learning for teachers: Capstone for educational reform* (pp. 73–83). Ann Arbor, MI: Prakken.

Shaver, J. P. (1997). The past and future of social studies as citizenship education and of research on social studies. *Theory and Research in Social Education, 25,* 210–215.

Shaver, J. P., Davis, O. L., Jr., & Helburn, S. M. (1980). *An interpretive report on the status of precollege social studies education based on three NSF-funded studies.* Washington, DC: National Science Foundation.

Silberman, C. E. (1970). *Crisis in the classroom.* New York: Random House.

Singleton, H. W. (1980). Problems of Democracy: The revisionist plan for social studies education. *Theory and Research in Social Education, 8,* 89–104.

Smith, F. R. (1965). The curriculum. In B. G. Massialas & F. R. Smith (Eds.), *New challenges in the social studies: Implications of research for teaching* (pp. 21–61). Belmont, CA: Wadsworth.

Smith, F. R., & Cox, C. B. (1969). *New strategies and curriculum in social studies.* Chicago: Rand McNally.

Snedden, D. (1935). The effect upon methods of a changing curriculum: With special reference to the social studies. In E. B. Wesley (Ed.), *The historical approach to methods of teaching the social studies* (pp. 9–19). Philadelphia: McKinley.

Snyder, S. (2003, October 9). City eager for students to get wiser with money. *Philadephia Inquirer.*

Soltis, J. F. (1968). *An introduction to the analysis of educational con-*

cepts. Reading, MA: Addison-Wesley.

Sosniak, L. A. (1999). Professional and subject matter knowledge for teacher education. In G. A. Griffin (Ed.), *The education of teachers* (pp. 185–204). Chicago: National Society for the Study of Education.

Stigler, J. W., & Hiebert, J. (1999). *The teaching gap: Best ideas from the world's teachers for improving education in the classroom.* New York: Free Press.

Stodolsky, S. S. (1988). *The subject matters: Classroom activity in math and social studies.* Chicago: University of Chicago Press.

Stodolsky, S. S., Salk, S., & Glaessner, B. (1991). Student views about learning math and social studies. *American Educational Research Journal, 28,* 89–116.

Superka, D. P., & Hawke, S. D. (1982). Social roles: A focus for social studies in the 1980s. In I. Morrissett (Ed.), *Social studies in the 1980s* (pp. 118–130). Alexandria, VA: Association for Supervision and Curriculum Development.

Sutcliff, R. (1994). *The lantern bearers.* New York: Sunburst.

Switzer, T. J. (1993). In retrospect: Sociological Resources for the Social Studies curriculum project. *The Social Studies, 84,* 224–229.

Thornton, S. J. (1988). Curriculum consonance in United States history classrooms. *Journal of Curriculum and Supervision, 3,* 308–320.

Thornton, S. J. (1990). Should we be teaching more history? *Theory and Research in Social Education, 18,* 53–60.

Thornton, S. J. (1991). Teacher as curricular-instructional gatekeeper in social studies. In J. P. Shaver (Ed.), *Handbook of research on social studies teaching and learning* (pp. 237–248). New York: Macmillan.

Thornton, S. J. (1993). Toward the desirable in social studies teaching. In J. Brophy (Ed.), *Advances in research on teaching: Vol. 4. Case studies of teaching and learning in social studies* (pp. 157–178). Greenwich, CT: JAI Press.

Thornton, S. J. (1994). The social studies near century's end: Reconsidering patterns of curriculum and instruction. In L. Darling-Hammond (Ed.), *Review of Research in Education, 20* (pp. 223–254). Washington, DC: American Educational Research Association.

Thornton, S. J. (1996). NCSS: The early years. In O. L. Davis, Jr. (Ed.), *NCSS in retrospect* (pp. 1–7). Washington DC: National Council for the Social Studies.

Thornton, S. J. (2001a). Educating the educators: Rethinking subject matter and methods. *Theory into Practice, 40,* 72–78.

Thornton, S. J. (2001b). From content to subject matter. *The Social Studies, 92,* 237–242.

Thornton, S. J. (2001c). Legitimacy in the social studies curriculum. In L. Corno (Ed.), *A century of study in education: The centennial volume* (pp. 185–204). Chicago: National Society for the Study of Education.

Thornton, S. J. (2001d). Subject specific teaching methods: History. In J.

Brophy (Ed.), *Subject-specific teaching methods and activities* (pp. 291–314). Oxford: Elsevier Science.

Thornton, S. J. (2002). Does everybody count as human? *Theory and Research in Social Education, 30,* 178–189.

Thornton, S. J. (2004a). Citizenship education and social studies curriculum change after 9/11. In C. Woyshner, J. Watras, & M. S. Crocco (Eds.), *Social education in the twentieth century: Curriculum and context for citizenship* (pp. 210–220). New York: Peter Lang.

Thornton, S. J. (2004b). School reform and social studies possibilities. In P. B. Uhrmacher & J. Matthews (Eds.), Intricate palette: Working the ideas of Elliot Eisner (pp. 183–195). Upper Saddle River, NJ: Pearson.

Thornton, S. J. (in press). Incorporating internationalism into the social studies curriculum. In N. Noddings (Ed.), *Educating global citizens: Challenges and opportunities.* New York: Teachers College Press.

Thornton, S. J., & Wenger, R. N. (1990). Geography curriculum and instruction in three fourth-grade classrooms. *Elementary School Journal, 90,* 515–531.

Thursfield, R. E. (Ed.). (1947). *The study and teaching of American history.* Washington, DC: National Council for the Social Studies.

Tyler, R. W. (1949). *Basic principles of curriculum and instruction.* Chicago: University of Chicago Press.

Valenzuela, A. (1999). *Subtractive schooling: U.S.-Mexican youth and the politics of caring.* Albany: State University of New York Press.

Vanaria, L. M. (1958). *The National Council for the Social Studies: A voluntary organization for professional service.* Unpublished doctoral dissertation, Columbia University, New York.

Walker, D. F. (1979). Approaches to curriculum development. In J. Schaffarzick & G. Sykes (Eds.), *Value conflicts and curriculum issues* (pp. 263–290). Berkeley, CA: McCutchan.

Walker, D. F. (2003). *Fundamentals of curriculum* (2nd ed.). Mahwah, NJ: Erlbaum.

Watras, J. (2002). Debating the curriculum: Social studies or history, 1892–1937. *The Social Studies, 93,* 245–250.

Watras, J. (2004). Historians and social studies educators, 1893–1998. In C. Woyshner, J. Watras, & M. S. Crocco (Eds.), *Social education in the twentieth century: Curriculum and context for citizenship* (pp. 192–209). New York: Peter Lang.

Weiler, K. (1999). The struggle for democratic public schools in California: Helen Hefferan and Corinne Seeds. In M.S. Crocco, P. Munro, & K. Weiler (Eds.), *Pedagogies of resistance: Women educator activists, 1880–1960* (pp. 83–114). New York: Teachers College Press.

Weinthal, E. (2002). *State making and environmental cooperation: Linking domestic and international politics in Central Asia.* Cambridge: MIT Press.

Wesley, E. B. (1943). History in the school curriculum. *Mississippi Valley Historical Review, 29,* 565–575.

Wesley, E. B. (1944). *American history in schools and colleges: The report of the Committee on American History in Schools and Colleges of the American Historical Association, the Mississippi Valley Historical Association, the National Council for the Social Studies.* New York: Macmillan.

Wesley, E. B. (1967). Let's abolish history courses. *Phi Delta Kappan, 49,* 3–8.

Whelan, M. (1991). James Harvey Robinson, the new history, and the 1916 social studies report. *The History Teacher, 24,* 191–202.

White, J. J. (1986). Decision-making with an integrative curriculum. *Childhood Education, 62,* 337–343.

White, J. J. (1987). The teacher as broker of scholarly knowledge. *Journal of Teacher Education, 38*(4), 19–24.

White, J. J. (1988). Searching for substantial knowledge in social studies texts. *Theory and Research in Social Education, 16,* 115–140.

White, J. J., & Rumsey, S. (1993). Teaching for understanding in a third-grade geography lesson. In J. Brophy (Ed.), *Advances in research on teaching, Vol. 4: Case studies of teaching and learning in social studies* (pp. 33–69). Greenwich, CT: JAI Press.

Whitehead, A. N. (1929). *The aims of education and other essays.* New York: Macmillan.

Whitson, J. A. (2004). What social studies teachers need to know: The new urgency of some old disputes. In S. Adler (Ed.), Critical issues in social studies teacher education (pp. 9–35). Greenwich, CT: Information Age.

Wilentz, S. (1997, April 20). The past is not a "process." *The New York Times.*

Wilson, S. M., & McDiarmid, G. W. (1996). Something old, something new: What do social studies teachers need to know? In F. B. Murray (Ed.), *The teacher educator's handbook: Building a knowledge base for the preparation of teachers* (pp. 295–319). San Francisco: Jossey-Bass.

World regions. (2003). Orlando, FL: Harcourt.

Zumwalt, K. K. (1989). Beginning professional teachers: The need for a curricular vision of teaching. In M. C. Reynolds (Ed.), *Knowledge base for the beginning teacher* (pp. 173–184). Oxford: Pergamon Press.

Index

Academic goals, 59–61
Adler, Mortimer, 55
A Farewell to Arms (Hemingway),
105
Aims, vii–ix. See also Goals
aims talk, 17–22, 45–47
and goals and objectives, 45–47,
57
scholarship as a source, 54–56
society as a source, 52–54
students as a source, 48–52
American Historical Association
(AHA), 21–22, 28–29, 34, 38,
40–41
Aptitude, 51–52
Aral Sea, 70–71, 84, 87
Association of American
Geographers, 29, 31

Barton, Keith, 98
*Basic Principles of Curriculum and
Instruction* (Tyler), 58
Beard, Charles, 7
Bennett, William, 17–18
Bernstein, Basil, 3
Big ideas, 86–87
Bowman, Isaiah, 26
Broker of scholarly knowledge, 55
Brophy, Jere, 10
Bruner, Jerome, 49
Business education, 61

Cheney, Lynne, 4
Choice, ix, 25, 50–52
and continuity, ix, 64–65
and interests, ix, 50, 65
Citizenship, 6, 22, 23–24, 37, 39–40,

45–46, 54, 55–56, 60, 77
Civics, 23, 30, 63, 77–78
Commission on the Social Studies
(AHA), 41
Committee of Seven (AHA), 21–22,
28–29
and method, 75
Committee of Ten (NEA), 19–23
Committee on American History,
34–38
Committee on Social Studies,
21–24, 52
and Committee of Ten, 21–24
and Committee on American
History, 37
and methods of teaching, 75–76
and Problems of Democracy,
39–40
Controversy, 52, 54
Cronbach, Lee, 85
Cultural literacy, 17–18
Curriculum development, 60–61,
73–77
and aims, vii–ix, 45–56
beginning point for, 30–32
deliberative platform for, 68
generic, 76
and goals, 59–66
interdisciplinary, 103, 106
as policymaking, 75–76
problem-centered, ix, 42–43
and social class, 53
site-specific, 70
systematic, 73–74
and teachers, vii–ix, 58, 68–69,
101–103
Curriculum potential, 6, 10–11, 68,

About the Author

Stephen J. Thornton is Associate Professor of Social Studies and Education at Teachers College, Columbia University. For 6 years he taught social studies and English at the middle- and high-school levels. He continues to be intrigued by how teachers decide what is worth teaching and how it might be effectively taught. His publications have focused on the ramifications of these decisions by social studies teachers for curriculum improvement, instruction, and teacher education.